Dedication

This book is dedicated to James Kraft, one of our Senior Scribes who has contributed so much to the class with his positive outlook, joyful disposition and thoughtful and humorous essays on life.

Introduction

When I began facilitating the Moreno Valley Life Story/Creative Writing Class several years ago, I had no idea that it would result in not one, but two collections of our work. In our first anthology, **_Aged to Perfection_**, we included recollections, personal reflections, observations about life, past experiences, words of wisdom, and, of course, our creative endeavors. While many of those participants are in this new anthology, some have moved on and new ones have taken their place.

During those years, we've shared all types of writing- stories from childhood, poignant stories about friends, relatives, significant people who passed through our lives and left indelible impressions; travel adventures, short stories, essays and poems. What better way to continue to showcase our creative endeavors than to put together another anthology featuring a small sample of our efforts; hence, **_Aged to Perfection 2_**. Like our first anthology, the contributions in this book include life lessons learned, trials and tribulations, challenges, words of encouragement, tributes, stories that made us laugh, and touched our lives. It has been an enjoyable and an enlightening and experience for me.

Anna Christian

6

CONTENTS BY TITLE

CONTENTS BY AUTHOR

10

A Coin
Mona Lisa Stallworth

Round and shiny. Found all around
Not worth much on the open market

The least of all coins is a penny, which is never sought after except –when one comes upon a wishing fountain. The sight of a wishing fountain causes even the most dignified to go scouring through their pocket or purse in search of a coin. Yes, at a wishing fountain a coin becomes a very valuable commodity. There are no loose coins on the ground near a wishing fountain. For we all know, a coin is the only key to having a wish answered.

Isn't it a wonder how something that once lacked great value is now sought after? Could the same be said of us? Until we see life as our fountain and our gifts, talent and skills as the keys that open up a whole world of possibilities – many walk around aimlessly feeling as though they have no real value; incapable of doing anything great.

May I make a suggestion, my friend? Let's pretend we have all the coins we need and they represent our thoughts, ideas, inventions and dreams. Let's throw them into the wishing fountain of life with the belief that whatever we wished for will come true and then watch to see how many of our thoughts, ideas, inventions and dreams will truly come to pass!

A Day in Grandmother's Kitchen

Anna Chase

My grandmother's kitchen was a feast for the senses that day.

She must have started early, because the sauce was already bubbling away on the stovetop, made with her own canned tomatoes, simmering in the big enamel pot with chunks of meat and her special blend of herbs and spices. I lifted the lid to take a whiff. It was a beautiful thing to behold. Ah! the aroma! My favorite smell in all the world.

On the counter I saw her well-worn basket heaped to overflowing with a bounty of vegetables fresh from the garden. It was like a still life painting in my frame of vision. A masterwork of nature! Bright red tomatoes, smooth and round as a baby's bottom; shiny eggplant, like a giant purple pear; sun kissed peppers streaked in green, yellow and red, not quite ready to be one or the other; long strands of green beans draped over the top. Lying alongside, right on the counter, were piles of leafy green parsley, smelling like freshly mowed grass and stems of bright green basil with the scent of fresh earth still clinging.

On the opposite counter sat a thick heavy bowl – the old-fashioned kind with pink roses on a cream-colored background. I could almost see the bread dough rising under the towel. When I lifted the towel the smell was yeasty and sweet. I could almost taste it in the back of my throat.

While I waited for grandma, I sat on the wooden kitchen stool imagining the meal we would prepare. When she comes, she will kiss my cheek and call me "figlia mia", which literally means "my daughter". Then she'll dip a piece of yesterday's bread in the sauce to give me a taste. Then she'll send me to the sink to wash my hands and we will begin to prepare the meal.

She tells me to punch the dough down, gently with my fists the way she taught me, so that it can rise a second time. I can hear and feel the wisp of air as it escapes from the dough as it sinks to the bottom of the bowl. When it rises again, we will pull pieces off and shape them into rolls, which we will place on a baking sheet, cover with a kitchen towel and leave to rise a final time before baking.

Grandma blanches the green beans in boiling water, drains them and sets them aside to cool for a salad. She slices the eggplant into thick rounds, and then shows me how to set up the breading station. She gets three shallow bowls from the cupboard and instructs me to put some flour in one. Then she lets me crack a couple of eggs in the second bowl. I beat them with a fork; then we pour some breadcrumbs and grated Parmesan cheese in the third bowl. Grandma demonstrates how to dip each piece of eggplant; first in the flour, next in the egg, then in the breadcrumbs and cheese, and then she leaves me to it. I place the breaded slices on a large platter and Grandma fries them up in a large cast iron skillet until they are crisp and golden. Once drained on paper towels, they are put into a warm oven to keep until the rest of the meal is prepared.

Next she slices those beautiful multi-colored peppers and fries them up with some of Grandpa's homemade Italian sausage. The aroma is making me crazy for a taste. I don't think I have ever smelled anything quite so wonderful, except for the sauce, of course!

Now for the fresh tomato and green bean salad. Grandma slices up the juicy red ripe tomatoes and adds them to the green beans with some chopped garlic. She instructs me to tear up some of the fresh basil and parsley to sprinkle over the top. She says it's better to tear fresh herbs, rather than chop them. The salad is dressed very simply with salt, pepper and extra virgin olive oil.

Now the pasta goes into the boiling water and the rolls go into the oven. I can't wait!

When everything is ready, grandma asks me to call everyone to the table, and with a little help from my aunts, we arrange everything on the big round table in the dining room.

As always, Grandpa has a jug of homemade wine sitting on the floor by his chair.

We bow our heads as Grandma leads us in a prayer of thanks and gratitude for our loved ones around the table and for the bounty of delicious homegrown food.

Some of my most cherished memories are of the times I spent in my grandmother's kitchen. I learned the Italian way of cooking with simple fresh ingredients prepared with love.

A Rose by Any Other Name

Karen (Kay) Donner

Some things never change or do so ever so slowly that one doesn't notice. Some things change seemingly right before my eyes. My husband picked a rose bud from his garden the other day and set it on my pillow so that I would only see it upon retiring that evening. How lovely was that gesture! As you might imagine, the rose opened its petals, gave off a beautiful aroma for the next few days and then withered away into a droopy blob. Yes, the rose changed drastically, but the rose itself and the romantic aura it released has remained the same since its beauty and fragrance was discovered.

I'm ironing my husband's shirts and I am aware that I don't have to sprinkle them. I remember sprinkling Dad's shirts, rolling them up, waiting a few hours and then ironing them. Those that were starched were more difficult to iron than those that were not. Well, I still have to iron the shirts – that hasn't changed, but I use a spray iron and spray starch if needed: so much easier. I have noticed that for a price I can't afford, I may purchase non-iron, no starch needed shirts. There's a nice change (except for the cost). However, there doesn't seem to be much change in the function of the ironing board itself. I don't remember before electric irons, but if you can think way back then, you have really noticed some change.

How about the television I'm watching while I iron? Holy-moley, what a difference a decade makes. Okay, maybe more like six decades. The "clicker" was invented; instead of seven channels, I have a multitude to select from. The darn thing will even record programs I might miss. Programs were entertaining and family oriented years ago. I remember the first shocking news televised was about the rescue of a small girl who had fallen into an uncovered and abandoned well. Today, I can view live terrorist activity, sexually oriented dramas, untold murder events, and various vocal and violent demonstrations. I recall the television screen was convex and small even though the housing was monstrous. Of course black and white were the colors of the day. The trick was to turn the "rabbit ears" or the roof top antenna to just the right setting to get a really clear picture. There have been so many changes to TV (yes, even the word television changed) that I am at a loss as to what I have, want, or need.

Now, here is something that has changed so rapidly that I never was able to get past square one. The telephone left me behind. Yes, grandma had the crank telephone; my mom and dad had a rotary. When we purchased the Princess phone, my sisters and I felt like we were so privileged. Our party line kept us from speaking for more than ten minutes at a time. We never would have thought about typing words (texting) to our friends no matter what the time of day or night.

So telephones today are in cars, on wrists, and in pockets, but almost never on our desks at home.

The microwave is, or was, novel. My mother got one in her apartment before I relented and bought one. I figured I'd get too lazy in the kitchen. I was right again! The stove has changed a little, but not so much that one would marvel at the complexity of the product. I equate it with the changes in refrigeration. As soon as electricity came into our lives, blocks of ice became scarce and the icebox was for camping trips only. Gosh, I used to love to run up to that ice delivery truck and swoop out the chips of ice.

Delivery trucks were so common. I salivated as the Helm's man pulled shelves from his truck. Those shelves were filled with delectable donuts, pies, bread, and other tempting goodies. The ice-cream man in his little wagon offered popsicles and ice cream bars. If my family wanted larger quantities of already made ice cream, we would stop the Arden Ice Cream truck. Our creamy and delicious milk was fresh on our doorstep every other day. The Fuller Brush man and the insurance guy were so friendly that it seemed they became part of our family. The Avon Lady made a "killing" at our house because my mom, my three sisters and I just loved the "stuff".

My dad worked at a gas station; first at a Union Oil station, then later at a Standard station. What a great service has been lost to our neighborhoods and communities. I suppose many look at this "do it yourself situation" as a convenience, but I notice a whole way of life that has disappeared. Dad never became rich during his "career", but he gave many young men (and once in awhile a needy person) an entry-level type job. I sincerely think that all this progress has made us a nation that does not "belong" to community and neighborhood. These small community businesses were the connective tissue of our neighborhoods.

Well, I digress. I look back and notice all the changes. Some I don't mind. I still think I should feel as if I were 16 years old. My body KNOWS it's a few years older than that, so this change I think I don't like.

I can't imagine what time will leave behind and become a loss to our civilization. For better or for worse, time will also bring innovative ideas and useful changes. I hope I get to see some of them, but I also hope I will not be expected to utilize all of them. Learning the computer has been enough for any one of my age.

I will declare this. That rose left on my bed pillow and the meaning of ardor that it represents will forever remain on the top of the list for romance and love. It cannot be perfected!

Abalone Cove
Mary Maurry

Early Saturday mornings were always a surprise to us with the aroma of bacon, eggs and fried potatoes floating in the air making its way to our bedrooms. A whiff of hot chocolate and coffee perking on the stove was a hint that something else was brewing for the day. My brother Richard, my sister Margie and I would jump out of bed, get dressed, and run to the kitchen to have breakfast and listen to Mom and Dad talk about what was going to happen for the day.

We're going to the beach or as Dad would call it 'the rocks'. That meant we were going to the Palos Verdes Peninsula where Dad would take us to fish and catch Abalone. After a hardy breakfast we helped Dad pack the fishing poles, tackle and ice chest while Mom gathered her frying skillet, utensils, spices and needs where she packed them into a wooden box Dad made her for these trips.

It was a long ride going from Artesia to Palos Verdes. Back in the fifties the California freeways were not built to go straight through yet. We made the best of it and enjoyed riding in our dad's nineteen-forties two-door gray Chevrolet. We laughed and giggled, as it seemed to hit every bump in the road.

Driving through the Peninsula was like a fairy tale to me. We drove through the up and down winding roads that followed the natural structure of the land created by the pounding of the sea. There were also parts of beautiful trees along the rolling hills sometimes so tall that they grew together forming a tunnel over the road that are still there today. The homes and mansions were so beautiful that I would get lost in my imagination making my own fairytale. The sound of rocks crushing under Dad's tires and dust coming through the open windows broke me out of my thoughts.

We're here! We got out of the car and quickly helped to unload it. Here's where our real adventure started. We all had to carry something down the steep scary dirt trail to get to the water. It was so steep that my sister and I would sit down and slide on our rear ends dragging the empty ice chest. When we got to the bottom we had to climb over rocky terrain to get to Dad's favorite spot where the fishing was good and the abalone was in abundance. As Mom and Dad set up camp for the day, we jumped into the cold pools of water left by the outgoing waves, rinsing off the dust covering us from head to toe. We laid out our clothes to dry on the surrounding rocks; we had our bathing suits under our clothes.

In the meantime, Dad pumped up the inner tubes and tied on the nets where we would put our catch later. We used the tubes to float on as the waves pushed us in like being on a surfboard. After a little fun we started looking for that delicious tasting abalone. The water was so clear that we could see them stuck on the rocks. Dad made us steel-like crowbars and taught us how to pry them off the rocks and put them in the nets tied to our tubes. It was fun diving below the water holding our breath to see all the beautiful sea flowers, while searching for our catch.

After collecting the abalones, Dad would size them and make sure they were legal to take. He'd clean them and give them to Mom who already had a little fire going with the skillet ready to cook them. She sliced them up and using the spices she brought, she made a delicious meal for us as we enjoyed the beautiful purely colorful shells (left from the not needed abalone). We then packed up and readied ourselves for the steep climb back up the scary hill back to the car. As kids would, we slept all the way home.

Sunday morning after church we took the shells we brought home, made decorations for our patio, and enjoyed remembrances of our adventure at the rocks.

That trail is still there today

Adam
Jain Householder

Adam is my nephew; a doe-eyed, freckle-faced little boy; the youngest of my sister Christine's four boys. There were eight boys in all including three of my own, and one from my sister, Lynn. Within a thirteen-year period we had put together a clan of cousins that were connected to each other throughout their growing-up years.

They were a boisterous bunch of untapped testosterone-little running legs attached to feet with untied shoes; dirty faces and sweat-drenched hair and Kool-aid spilled down the fronts of their shirts; barn doors always left open in haste to get back outside; guns and forts and playing in the creek; bikes and bruises, tears and laughter; rumbling and tumbling; action that never stopped. How lucky we were when we had them all together.

I remember one Christmas Eve when someone had heard on the radio that Santa was spotted overhead in our area. I can still see the wide-eyed looks on all their faces as they heard the news. Then all we saw was the backs of their little-boy haircuts as they scurried off toward the bedroom where my sister had put their bunk beds right in front of the window. Their noses and cheeks were pressed tightly against the glass trying to get a glimpse of a sled or a reindeer. Some of them were sure they saw him; the others straining in the direction of pointing fingers for any clue of Santa. The excitement was indescribable.

Years go by. The older we get, the quicker we seem to travel through this life. Our memories are there and we intend to go back and visit, but we seem to get swept in other directions.

We went to Adam's funeral today, the sweet, doe-eyed, freckle-faced son of my sister, Christine. The father of a 3-year-old son of his own, Adam would have been 28 next month. He was an avid motocross rider. He died on his motorcycle, doing something that he had a passion for. We try to find some peace in that, but it only detracts us for a few seconds. One of our boys is gone ... the unthinkable has happened to our family. All of our living, all of our different directions have come to a halt, and we are together again. All eight boys are there. Only this time, one is in a box and seven stand crying and holding on to each other. The oldest is now almost forty. All of a sudden we see that they are men, these children of ours, and our hearts ache to see them all running around again, dirty-faced and laughing, with Kool-aid spilled down the fronts of their shirts. We cry for Adam ... and we cry for the seven standing ... and we cry for what has come and gone from our lives.

Adventures of a Tooth
Ollie Eubany

Years ago before root canal and crowns you went to the dentist for fillings or extractions. Now I have more crowns and root canals that it is hard to find an original tooth in my mouth. For years I only needed a cleaning on my six monthly visits although there were some years of lapse.

Three years ago the dentist pronounced that I would need a root canal on my left upper tooth. I could not imagine why since I was just having a little pain when I chewed on that side and after all it was a root canal and how do you do a root canal on top of a root canal. For that reason I did not go back and a year later I went to a different dental office, which drew me because of the office title, Gentle Dental. I saw the dentist who said as long as I did not have any pain I could just buy heavy floss and just floss that tooth after every meal. A few months later my company cancelled dental insurance for all retirees and I had to find another dentist who accepted Medicare. I then chose Happy Dental, such a happy title. This was a year later and Happy Dental referred me to their specialist in Riverside. When I arrived at that office the oral surgeon said the original owner had died and he was just taking over. He took a look at my tooth and said it would be difficult and would take a long time to do a root canal on that tooth. I then thanked him and left.

A few months later I went back to Happy Dental and saw the hygienist. She took x-rays on only eight of my front teeth up and down and told me I needed a deep cleaning on my teeth, and after tabulation she said it would cost me $1900. She never mentioned the root canal I had been told I needed, so now I was in search of a new dentist.

Two years later I chose Smile Right dental office and by then I was really in pain. The dentist said my tooth had rotted to the root and I would have to see a specialist. I called my provider, Delta Insurance. They referred me to a specialist to have the tooth removed. Only thing was the specialist I was referred to was in Sun City and I live in Moreno Valley and no way was I taking my pain to Sun City. I called my insurance company again and they referred me to an oral surgeon across from Smile Right so I made an appointment with that office by phone. When I saw the Specialist there, he said he would not pull the tooth since my referral letter was for Sun City and that my letter only referred me for consultation and I should go back to Smile Right to have the dentist give them a letter confirming I needed this tooth pulled. They had tried at first to contact Smile Right to have them fax over authorization but by then Smile Right office had closed for lunch. An hour later I rushed back to Smile Right and they said they could not give me a referral since their dentist had gone home.

Meantime that morning Smile Right had taken my partial and sent it out to have a tooth added in the place of the tooth to be pulled and the tooth had already been added to the partial. It would cost me to remove the new tooth and pay again to have it put back. I hurried across to the oral surgeon's office to explain this to them but the lady at the desk told me the specialist only came in on Thursday and he had gone home since he had no more patients. I then went back to Smile Right and I was not smiling as I demanded my partial returned to me. There was another person at the desk this time, a middle age woman. She said she could refer me to a private dentist nearby on Sunnymead Ave. if I could pay to have the tooth pulled.

She promptly called that office after I told her I would pay. She made an appointment with them for the following morning and she promised that my partial would be ready afterward. I decided to go immediately to the office on Sunnymead. When I reached that office I explained to the lady what I had been going through. She said the dentist could remove my tooth right away. I then asked if I could be put under and she said I would need a letter from my health provider, my medical doctor. At any rate by this time I prepared myself and the tooth was pulled and I felt like my jaw would break, and the next day I went back to Smile Right and now I have my dentures.

Aging Gracefully & Gratefully
Anna Chase

There's a quote that says:
"It's not how old you are, it's how you are old."

Aging gracefully isn't easy but keeping a positive attitude can make all the difference. Our society focuses too much on the negative aspects of aging, and dwelling on it can drive you crazy. After all, if you sit around moping about getting older and how your time is running out, you will be cheating yourself out of the time you have left.

Aside from a positive attitude, being flexible is also important. Those who have been the most flexible throughout their lives will be better equipped to move through the ongoing changes of aging.

If we see these natural changes in health, decreasing energy, aches and pains and so forth in a very negative way, it will add a lot of unnecessary stress to our lives. Rigid thinkers will have a much harder time accepting the inevitable changes of aging.

However, not all seniors are pessimistic. Even though they tire more easily and have to take things slower, the more optimistic ones manage to move through the emotional and physical challenges of aging with grace and gratitude.

Another quote states: "You don't stop laughing when you grow old, you grow old when you stop laughing." Keeping a sense of humor is another positive factor when it comes to aging.

Retirement can be an especially difficult time for many seniors, leaving them without a reason to get up in the morning. They may become depressed or feel that their lives no longer have meaning. This transition will be easier if they have cultivated areas of interest other than their work, well before retirement. That way, they don't just stop working one day and simply wait for the end; rather it can be a time to follow their passions and cultivate new interests and activities.

Part of aging happily is finding activities that are important to you, such as travel, hobbies, spiritual growth and many other areas of lifelong learning. Continuing to learn and grow is of prime importance to aging well. Now that you have the time, even if you don't have much money, there are many things to pursue that can keep you interested in life and give you a renewed passion and desire to get up and get going.

A continuing sense of purpose is most important. For me, it helps to mentally review my day each evening and to visualize what I plan to do the next day. Maybe it's my scheduled day at the gym, or I have a new book to start; even something as seemingly mundane as what specific portion of the house I'm planning to clean; so when I wake up in the morning I already have a plan and ultimately a sense of accomplishment. Of course, if a more exciting opportunity presents itself, and if I'm flexible, I can always change my plans.

Obviously, great change comes with aging. We may eventually lose our independence and may have to depend on others to help us. With few exceptions, we will probably not be living alone, driving to the grocery store or walking as far as we used to.

If you live well into your 90s, you've probably been blessed with good luck or good genes, and you've dodged a few bullets. The fact that you haven't died from a fatal accident or a premature disease, things that take the lives of much younger people, is something for which to be thankful.

Aging is inevitable. We are all getting a little bit older each day from the moment we're born. While it's true that aging brings certain hardships, we must keep in mind that the old are a select group of survivors. As we age, we hopefully gain wisdom, insight and resilience, but the mere fact of living to a ripe old age is, in itself, an accomplishment.

Ultimately, we can look at each passing day as time running out, or we can look at each new day as a rebirth and renewal of life to be savored and appreciated.

Cason
Ollie Eubany

Cason was nine years old when his family moved to the US from a small village in Nigeria. His mother is American while his father was Nigerian so the family had no difficulty getting into the US.

They settled in Los Angeles and moved in with Cason's uncle, his father's brother in a three-bedroom apartment located off Beverly Blvd. His mother got admission for Cason in the elementary school on Grove St. His sister Janet who was two years older than Cason was admitted to Venice HS Magnet and met her bus every day on Vermont Ave. while Cason's mom drove him to school every morning.

On his first day Cason was very nervous as his mother took him to the principal's office and told the principal that it was Cason's first time in the US and he had completed 6th grade previously in West Africa but she wanted him to adjust before going to junior high school. The principal told her to leave him with her since she was going to take him to his class and introduce him to his teacher.

It was vey hard for Cason that first day since he had a very strong accent and he could sense the other children laughing at him. The teacher liked him since he would raise his hand and when acknowledged he would stand up with answers to her questions. After class these two boys came up to him, pushed him and started teasing him because of his accent. He had to fight these two boys everyday of the term he was in school but he never complained to his mother. He graduated and went to Griffith Magnet Jr. High School in East Los Angeles.

In his new school things went so much better for him since there were more children from Mexico and other countries, and he was able to make friends whom he is still in touch with today. Upon graduating he went to North Hollywood Zoo Magnet while his family moved to North Hollywood. By now Cason was 6'2 and had lost most of his accent. He got his mother to buy him pairs of jeans size 56 so they could sag on him. He also started wearing his baseball cap backward. He now was very cool. He had a circle of friends; two were with him in the Zoo Magnet at Griffith Park where he had his magnet subjects.

One afternoon, after class as he was chilling with his friends, he saw coming toward him one of the boys who had fought with him in the 6th grade. Cason walked up to him and said, "What's up? Do I know you?" The boy looked up at him and said in a small voice, "Hi" then ran off.

After a few weeks in high school, Cason told his mother he wanted a tattoo and he also wanted to pierce his ears. "No!" said his mother. "You will never do that." What did Cason do? When his older sister came home that weekend he had her corn roll his hair and he wore it like that throughout his years in high school. His father had an ornamental walking stick that Cason would take to school every day. He was really COOL now.

He graduated with honors from North Hollywood

Zoo Magnet and attended UC Irvine (with his hat on forward. Upon graduation from UC Irvine he went on to Hasting Law School in San Francisco. Today he is an Attorney and works for a firm in Redlands. He is married and has a son.

Dad
Vivian Pleasant

What happened between you and Mom
is still a mystery to me.
I guess that I shall never see
The things that happen
between a woman and a man.
I guess that I will never understand.
As I grew I knew there was a missing link
Wouldn't you know that's what I'd come
to think.
As time passed I began to wonder
Exactly where was he asunder
Do I have his ears, nose or eyes?
I know now; definitely not his thighs.
Will I ever see him, I'd say?
And then God said, "Perhaps, someday"
And when he cast his eyes my way
Will I know exactly what to say?

Embrace Love
Regina Crump

Love is evolving every moment, so don't divert or reject it with excuses and judgment. Find being fulfilled sufficient in your companionships and relationships that come from unconditional liking. Beauty can be seen in your life when you close the door to negativity.

Love is evolving every second; so do find laughter in every sense of the sound. To hear another's explosive joy will move you almost to tears, with each different tone. You can't escape what it does to the heart. Isn't God smart?

Love is evolving so don't wait an hour to embark on life's best things to flower. Improvise and maneuver what you must to participate in what is only here for a short length of time.

Excuses, Excuses

Anna Chase

Sometimes I catch myself making excuses for not doing something I know I should do, like exercising, for instance. I can always come up with some excuse or other for not going to the gym or taking that walk that I know would be good for me. I don't make these excuses out loud to anyone else, but quietly in my mind to myself.

That little voice might say, 'I'm just too tired this morning because I didn't get a good night's sleep. I shouldn't have stayed up so late watching that movie. Maybe I'll go later, after the coffee kicks in.'

Then, after I've made and accepted the first excuse, the others just follow naturally.

Okay, now I've had my coffee and I conveniently remember that my neighbor and exercise partner is out of town. Do I want to go it alone? Maybe it won't be so bad if I have my iPod. But wait, I think I forgot to charge it and the treadmill is so boring without someone to talk to or my music. Okay, I can afford to skip the gym today. I'll just do some aerobics at home and use my hand weights – right after lunch.

Now lunch has come and gone and I notice that my bad knee is acting up again. What if those aerobics make it worse, then I won't be able to go to the gym tomorrow. Maybe I better take it easy today and give that knee a good rest. I can still take a walk outside later, before it gets dark.

So, I watch a little daytime TV and doze off in the process. I awake with a jolt and find out that I've slept through almost all of the Dr. Oz show. I'm just in time to hear him sign off by saying that exercise is the most important thing we can do to stay young and healthy. Now I'm really feeling guilty. Well, the day isn't over yet, I tell myself. I'll put on my shoes, walk to the mailbox and check out the weather for that walk, but after being warm and cozy inside, it feels cold and it's a little windy outside. I think I better skip the walk. I don't want to catch a cold!

Okay, what have I learned from this? Sometimes when I hear that first excuse starting to form, I quickly dismiss it and say to myself – "just do it," and off I go to the gym. However, it seems that once I accept that first excuse, I have already made up my mind to give it up for the day. So, rather than trying to rationalize it by making more excuses and feeling guilty all day, maybe I should just allow myself to take the day off without guilt with a vow to do better tomorrow.

Expect Changes
Alfred Turnbull

(An old man's guide to advanced age)

You are old Father William and your hair has become very white ... Lewis Carroll.

We are constantly told in the daily news reports that our population is aging. An advertisement in a popular magazine proclaims that 10,000 people turn 65 every day. They don't cite their research, but anyhow it is evident that there are a lot of children and a lot of old people around; also, there is evidence when you read obituaries in the newspaper that many people are living long lives. As one of the elder eldest (I am 89) I feel that I am in a position to expound on old age as an expert on how to exist in a hostile environment. At least I have some ideas and suggestions to those of you who are in your middle seventies and are going to have to be canny and realize that you are going to have to re-learn many things as time rushes by and you become among the old older.

First of all, particularly, if you are a man, you need a companion. Women seem to be stronger and more skillful in living by themselves. An old person needs to develop special skills to survive and care for themselves. A consultation with a physical therapist is worthwhile, for one must learn basic skills as how to sit and rise from a chair, get in and out of bed, walk and not shuffle, how to stand, how to get dressed, and how to move. Negotiating stairs is a huge problem if there is no railing or wall to balance oneself. A deep overstuffed chair or sofa could easily trap a person who no longer has strong pliable muscles to rise. There is a great need to have balancing skills to avoid falls.

After realizing and accommodating the unremitting physical limitations of aging, staying mentally alert is essential. Read the daily newspaper, books and magazines, do crossword puzzles, and learn to use a computer but beware of dangers that come with one; don't become enslaved to social networks and beware of people trying to scam you. Messages with weird or foreign words in the subject line should be consigned to the spam file. Learn to use the delete key. Form your own opinions, think for yourself, and avoid political pundits and preachers who demand your money to get you priority in heaven. Just because you are old you don't have to fall for some criminal's folderol!

Look after your health. Exercise daily, see your doctor when you are not feeling right, and visit your dentist; every tooth you keep adds a year to your longevity (this is my maxim). Your doctor, dentist and optometrist are vital guardians.

Another area you must consider as you age is your financial health. An absolute sign of dotage is squandering money. You do not have to contribute to every charity that sends you address labels and begs for cash. I feel giving to a scholarship fund at an accredited college is better than buying Thanksgiving dinner for the indolent. They will be hungry the day following. Absolutely never make loans or co-sign for a family member or friend. If a bank won't lend to them, you dare not. Run from financial advisors who want to sell insurance or dubious annuities. Find bonds and stocks to work for you and don't allow money to stay in a low yield bank account. Make a will that wisely distributes your estate and will not reward unworthy family members who never bother to call you, remember your birthday, or thank you for gifts as you become old.

Here are some additional ideas I have to offer

- Keep a supply of flashlights around: small, cheap, LED-type gives a lot of light and will save you in a power failure.
- Keep a light on in the bathroom.
- Be meticulous about taking your medications.
- Try not to cross roadways. You walk slowly and drivers are inattentive.
- Make friends.
- When out of your home, carry pepper spray to ward off muggers and pit bulls.
- Be a volunteer.
- Have a special place for your keys, eyeglasses, and other essentials. Immediate recall just about disappears as you go up in your 80's.
- Eat balanced meals and use fresh fruits for snacks.
- Take a short afternoon nap.
- Germs hate you. Fight them by washing your hands frequently and make liberal use of hand sanitizers when eating in buffets and restaurants.
- Graciously realize when you must surrender

your driver's license. When you leave, you don't want to take any pedestrians with you.

- Keep your doors locked, never answer your door after dark, and never admit a stranger into your home.
- Keep valuables and important papers in a safe deposit box. Be informed on local issues and vote.
- Pay your bills on line when possible. Go to the post office to mail checks.
- Be acquainted with your neighbors.
- Finally, be prudent and mature.

Father William, if you read on in Lewis Carroll's poem, was standing on his head. Accept that when you are in your 80s you must not do things that a child can. Don't be childish.

Four Feet and a Tail
Marcia P. Carter-Hill

Some people do not consider owning a pet. Many feel that it isn't necessary to incur the obligations and expense caring for an animal. If that is truly their feelings, then the subject is closed.

On the other hand, millions of people, worldwide, can't exist without a pet of some kind. That group supports a huge industry that I have been a part of for many years. Where dogs are the topic, I have been tested earning the title, *NDGAA Certified Master Groomer* since the early seventies.

For as long as I can remember there have been animals of some variety in and around all of my family members. Personally, the varieties have included, dogs, cats, many kinds of fish, canary birds, cockatiels, a little green lizard, one guinea pig, and a small rabbit. I sometimes wonder, why is this rather common all over the world?

All ages and genders seem to gravitate toward animals, admiring their beauty whether fur, feather, fin, hide or scale. It just seems natural. Why do we take the children to circuses, zoo's, Sea World, fairs, farms, and some go on safaris in foreign countries. The tendency to want to touch, caress, talk to gently, telling them how beautiful they are while looking into their eyes is the human response to show love and affection to many of earth's creatures. Documentaries reveal the many people that indulge in the same way to undomesticated wild animals. I will leave this to others, as I remain a faithful pup and kitten lover.

In America the dog and cat population seems to continually grow with most households having one of each or more of one kind or the other. The tendency to fall in love with a fluffy puppy or kitten and the desire to provide for its needs is almost uncontrollable. We instinctively need to protect and nurture them. We become emotionally unstable, just as much as we would be concerning a lost human baby. Not to mention the purchase price for some purebreds and exotics. You could consider adopting an older pet, a good choice for the elderly pet lover. Yet and still, it is a normal emotion. I am with you on this all the way.

My advice, though a little strict, is look before you leap! It would be wise to think about what commitment you are entering into. If you hadn't intentionally had a plan to acquire a pet for safety, company or pleasure, but, got caught up in seeing the animals that an individual had in a box at the shopping center, became overwhelmed looking at the adorable young creatures and lost control. WAIT, a few minutes, walk away from the scene, talk to yourself and evaluate the good and possible bad situation you will be getting involved with. There are many things for you to consider.

First, all babies grow up eventually. They may be little and cute now, but, how large will they become in six months to a year old? If the animal is a purebred, you might have done some research or worked with a breeder prior to shopping. You will at least have some information on what to expect in regards to size, personality, eventual color, and even inherited traits. That could include documented health issues. Good job!

The other side of the coin should be addressed if your heart has fallen for a designer or mixed breed. They can still be a wonderful pet, and will give the same joy and possible protection locked into their DNA, but wait, what are all of those different genes locked in the animal. Which ones will it display in time? You may be in for some surprises.

Next, is the decision to get the animal yours alone, or are other people in your life to be considered? Does it matter if it is male or female? Is your home or apartment right for a pet? Is there a yard for exercise or potty time? Must you have to take the animal out on walks, regardless of the weather? Can your budget afford licensing, shots, spaying or neutering, quality food, training, and boarding fees if you go on vacation? What if your animal is a noisy one, or your cat walks across your neighbors' car every morning! These ideas are not to discourage you, but to make you take time to evaluate your situation. If all is figured out, now you can better pick one out.

The act of caressing the soft and fluffy coats of some animals is very comforting to some people, but remember that hair has to have a great deal of care for the life of the animal. If you can do that chore yourself, great! If not, get it to the groomer on a steady routine basis. If you've selected a smooth or short hair breed, they still need a brushing and a nice bath on occasion. Yes, and all animals shed their hair one way or another. Curly coated ones shed into their own hair and it gets caught there needing frequent brushing to alleviate tangling and matting up. The smooth and short-haired ones dropping coat all over everything, especially during warmer weather. Think how you might take a sweater off because you feel too warm. Nature does that for warm-blooded animals. Now there's sweeping up!

For me, it's always been dogs that I love the most, my best friends and companions that I shared many wonderful, even exciting times together. Their eyes and ears on watch to protect, eager to learn and please, using their keen senses to understand my every emotion. Amusing me with their antics and playfulness. Sharing some tasty treats between us when visiting a drive thru. Giving me soft moans when I am sick or sad. Giving doggie hugs and little kisses to show their appreciation for the loving care I give them. They never say words of criticism and are loyal to their owner and family. What more could you ask for?

For sure, they are worth all we can give them because they give so much in return; the best friend to man, woman and child.

From Me To You

Regina Crump

I just happened to be venting my thoughts about a man when a dear person quoted to me, "If equal affection cannot be, let the most loving one be me." That right there slapped me in the face. I went a little further explaining how I felt this man didn't see me; he didn't hear me and acted like he didn't care about knowing me. What he did like was feeling my inside walls and my affectionate kisses.

Then I questioned my dearest friend, "Doesn't this man know that this kind of treatment brings about emotional disturbance in a woman's nature?" We both looked at each other with an expression of 'maybe not'.

I quoted what she said back to myself, and what it spoke to me was - when I speak the opposite language of my essence it tends to interrupt my development of beauty on the inside and for what corrupts my insides show on the outsides too. The next time the quote "If equal affection cannot be, let the most loving one be me;" it was used when I needed help with forgiveness.

As I contemplated what it meant to me, a lump rose up in my throat and my heart skipped a beat; it's amazing how words can affect how the body reacts and it really doesn't matter whether it was said in a harsh tone or not; what matters is where you are in the present and where you've been in the past.

You see the mind likes keeping memories around; sometimes the things that have been forgiven but not forgotten keep you in bondage, so I asked myself to stay free and leave room for God to fix what needs to be fixed; now whenever I feel a little prideful I use the quote "If equal affection cannot be, let the most loving one be me"; it reminds me to surrender to God's will, to stay humble and peaceful before Him.

Almighty God is here to give you strength; He empowers you to release whatever resentment you have harnessed up. Whatever offenses you have stored up, just be free to experience what he has planned for you; when you have passed the pitfalls of life, it will have no effect on your loving insides.

Stay focused on Jesus cause anything coming from Him; works for the good for who loves Him; and loves like Him.

Hanging Out With Hurt

Regina Crump

I've learned that when trying to help a person who's been hurt, it becomes the hardest thing to do. Because of the embedded attitudes the person carries, which make it hard to break through. If you are not equipped to protect yourself, you can become hurt in some way too.

If you are not mentally or physically strong and your heart is not of Christ, this project is over before it even starts. I know people can be hurt by the same things and be healed in different ways at different times, but when you move close to knowing Jesus you will see God's work in progress for your life.

I need your hurt to stop ruling; I want to be with you without negative thoughts of the past; God has allowed us to live through challenging times; for us to teach and demonstrate what it means to have family ties; Satan had his chance but we have overcome and our victory shows in our smile towards one another; along with laughter from silly jokes.

It's good while it lasts; but then you start remembering the pains of yesterday that's gone. I say to you stop reliving something in your mind that could only hurt you once; let's go on living well like we should. Satan has stolen and robbed us enough; God said you can't receive his daily bread if you stay full of old CRAP.

Have you dressed in a way that made you feel uncomfortable?
Mrs. Edith Nevins

Several years ago, my church sponsored a dinner dance at Town Gate Community Center in Moreno Valley. I was serving as a hostess stationed at the front door to receive the tickets and checks.

I wore a short-sleeve, two-piece hand knitted cranberry dress with pearl jewelry. As the church members and their husbands began arriving, I felt overdressed because many of the women were in casual clothes. I was not told that there was a dress code, I wore appropriate clothing for evening entertainment. I decided not to go back home to change my clothes.

Even though I felt uncomfortable with my dress, the music began and it changed my mood altogether. By the end of the evening, I had received many compliments from members about my outfit.

I drove home, pleased with myself for having worn one of my favorite evening outfits.

The older I get, I realize that I need to dress for my comfort level and disregard all the negative comments

Hobbies! Where Do I Start?
Mary Maurry

I recall starting my first hobby when I was about seven years old. Santa brought me a Dennis the Menace Doll for Christmas and I was determined to know all about his life. I watched every episode of Dennis on TV that I could and looked forward to Sundays when it was on. I was the youngest and last for everything. I anxiously waited for my turn to get the paper and rush to the cartoon section. There he was! Dennis, the Menace. My doll and I would lie on the floor and read all about Dennis's adventures. Then I carefully cut out his episode and stack it on top of those from past weeks in the bottom drawer of my dresser, reserved just for Dennis. The two stacks were already about three inches high.

Unfortunately, one-day Mom's friend carne to visit and brought her son with her while I was at school. That boy found Dennis and his clippings and tore them all to pieces and took my doll. It broke my heart and Dennis was gone. I could not bring myself to start over.

From then I went to collecting old wallets and broken watches. Well, that sucked! No money in those dirty old wallets and I couldn't tell time on "broken watches." I did save the watches and would figure out how to get the rubies and diamonds out of them later.

By the time I was about twelve I got my first

parrot. It was my parents but it only liked me. It talked a little. All it would say, when the phone rang, was: Hello, Hello, $1000.00 on White Face? You got it! I guess a bookie owned it before we did. My parents gave me the bird as long as I taught it something else to say. I did, like "good morning," "want coffee?" "Sugar?" and "May I help you?" Then I was able to sell it for twice what my parents bought it for.

I bought and sold parrots until one day one got out of its cage and chased my mother around the house and wouldn't let her out of the bathroom. It would screech at her every time she'd open the door and then it laughed, when she quickly closed it. You know that was the end of that hobby.

Life went on with no real hobbies until I was given an old box Brownie camera. I loved taking photos of anything and everything and to this day wouldn't you know it? I do have a collection of cameras, baseball cards, watches, coins, gems and many other things. AM I A PACK RAT? I have sold the coins and gems for extra income when I needed it. So, maybe I'm not a pack rat after all. I'm very organized.

When I retired, the company gave me a scholarship to go back to college. I took classes in Graphic Arts to learn to work with my photos, and later took a class in Photography. I learned enough to get honors on my photography, and even got a couple of my photos in the Museum of Photography in Riverside, California for three months. Then they went to the Museum of Palm Desert near Palm Springs for four months.

Having my photography in a museum made me a professional photographer. My photography has brought me an extra income over the last few years. It was well worth going back to school at sixty years of age.

NOW! Let's look at this:

A hobby is: *An activity or interest pursued for pleasure or relaxation.*

That's fine and dandy, but as I learned throughout the years and when you can see beyond that, it can turn into extra income. I learned from very young that there is always a way to make an extra dollar.

These days as we all know, our Social Security benefits and Retirement Pension just doesn't quite make it for all our needs in this economy. Why not earn a little from **pleasure and relaxation**! No need to stow it all away, just to be tossed later. I figure I can enjoy the fruits of my hobbies and creativity now.

I'VE DECIDED I WILL ALWAYS HAVE A HOBBY AND THUS CREATE MY LEGACY

How Do You Live Without Social Media?
Mrs. Edith Nevins

*Fit Form Watch, Twitter, E-Mail, Facebook,
Computer/Internet* (did I miss anything?)

When I moved into my retirement home twenty years ago, I made a specific choice not to have Social Media of any type in my house. My five sons had no choice but to accept my wishes. I have two phones in my house and I carry a cell phone.

To me, all forms of Social Media are an intrusion. I prefer to listen to the Christian Radio in the daytime and turn on television at 5 pm. I am an avid reader of books, newspapers and magazines. I have ordered the LA Times twice a week and receive the Press Enterprise four days a week.

For the past fourteen years, I have belonged to a Christian Book Club and have read all the books on a variety of topics. Also I find free books at Moreno Valley Senior Center. In the Moreno Valley Mall there is a bookstore that sells hard cover books for $2.00 and pocket books for $1.00. They also have sales, three books for $1.00. I take advantage of these sales to read different types of books.

I am active in my church and in a Non-Profit Organization. I am a Health Educator and for the past ten years,I have been making community presentations about breast cancer

My favorite past time is going to the movies at least one or twice a month. I enjoy watching the action on the big screen.

To me travel is fascinating and interesting, taking trips around the country to visit family and friends; finding new places to travel with family. Attending the graduation of grandchildren around the country keeps me in touch with family members. Funerals and family reunions run the gamut from sorrow to pleasure; memorable trips to Italy, visiting five cities, a ten day trip to Egypt with a three day cruise down the Nile River, and a trip to my mother's home in St. Kitts in the West Indies to celebrate my 72nd Birthday.

Five years of attendance at the Creative Writing Class has stimulated my brain to write on a variety of topics; I have two articles published in the 2014 anthology.

I live very well without Social Media using self-control and maintaining priorities over my life activities.

I Am A World Traveler
Mrs. Edith Nevins

I am a world traveler.
I wonder if the cruise will be enjoyable.
I hear music coming from the dining room.
I want to have a cabin with a porthole.

I am a world traveler.
I pretend to be rafting in Jamaica.
I feel the warm sun and water on my body.
I touch the raft to keep my balance.
I worry that I will fall into the water.
I cry if no one can help me.

I am a world traveler.
I understand that cruising on the Nile River
is relaxing.
I say to all, pay the money
and see for yourself.

I Dare You
Mona Lisa Stallworth

I dare you to live life to the fullest.
I dare you to dream the impossible dream.
I dare you to plan a glorious future.
I dare you to go beyond your wildest imagination.

I double dare you to use all your gifts,
talents and skills.
I double dare you to apply all the knowledge and
wisdom you have gained.
I double dare you to max out your creativity.
I double dare you to focus all your energy
on those things you excel at.

I triple dare you to help just one person.
I triple dare you to start a revolution.
I triple dare you to love instead of hate.
I triple dare you to believe you are God's masterpiece.

Yes, my friend, I am daring you to be the best person
you can be: taking off all limits.
Yes, I am daring you to care and do for others
and this earth.
Yes, my dear friend, I am daring you to be the **best**
human being you were created to Be!

They say the graveyard is the richest place on earth. Why you may ask? For in the graves lie inventions, businesses, books, stories, ideas and other riches never brought to the light of day. And maybe one of the reasons is the holders of such wealth were never challenged to do more, reach higher or value their inner vault of riches.

Well, today I challenge you all to dare to do and be more!
As long as you have breath it's not too late. Write, teach and share. Record, videotape and speak. With technology there are no limitations only excuses you use to delay until it's too late and you are gone with your treasures still intact.

It's in your control what do you say…
will you accept my dare today!

I Smell Them

Mary Touray

My mother, my sister,
Brother and my father
Dead, decaying lying in
Their shallow graves.

I smell their terror
Dead by the guns
Of my brother,
Different tribes,
Same color.

I smell the flies that
Swamped them,
laying eggs on them - me
As I sat beside them.

Too young, bewildered
To do otherwise
Their death-smell burns
My nose, my head.
The flies cover them and me
I smell them.
Can you
Tell me why?

Let Me Die, So I May Live
Mary Touray

If in dying I show a hatred for
White people and awake able to
Love myself and my ancestors
Then let me die.

If my dying takes the form of rejection
Of the opposite sex, yet I awake able to
Understand the pressure that we each
Experience trying so desperately
To be able Black men and women,
I prefer to die.

If in dying I am left insane
But awake understanding the real nature
Of my illness, then
Let me die.

If in dying I lash out and kill
But awake to accept my deed, then
Let me die.

If my dying as well as others enables
My brothers and sisters to unite into
A brotherhood, then
Let me die so others may live

Life is Art: Paint Your Dreams
Emma Jones

"Life is Art: Paint Your Dreams." The words on the tiny wooden plaque on the shelf in the shop caught my eye. I stared at it for a long time, reading the words over and over in my mind, and then I read them out loud. "Life is Art: Paint Your Dreams." The words were speaking to me. I placed the sign in my cart along with the other items and made my way to the checkout counter and paid for the items. I kept staring at the sign as the cashier placed it in the bag. "Life is Art: Paint Your Dreams" What does it really mean? I couldn't wait to get home and place the plaque on the fireplace mantle. When I got home, I got out the dictionary to see what Webster had to say.

Art - being creative; the making or doing things that have form and beauty.

Paint - a mixture of coloring matter, with oil, water used to coat a surface or make a picture.

Dreams - a series of thoughts, pictures or feelings that pass through the mind of a sleeping person.

a pleasant idea that one imagines or hopes for- to imagine as possible

Wow! If that is what that little sign was saying, I have been doing it all my life. I have a memory of myself when I was in the 7th grade art class. I love to paint. I was painting a picture of a man walking in the desert. The mood and expression of him that I was painting was that he was alone, had lost some of his clothes and the ones on his body were ragged, dirty, and torn. I had painted big drops of sweat falling from his face and his body was all bent over from the heat of his journey through the desert.

The art teacher approached my desk and studied my painting like she always did. She whispered, "Very good, Emma. When you get to high school take art."

When it was time for high school, I had to go to my counselor. I was counseled not to take art but to take business courses which I didn't like. I was more of an art and literature type person. I wanted to read books and write poetry and most of all to paint.

I stopped painting and listened to the advice of my counselor instead of the dream in my heart. Well, business courses did not prepare me for life. I struggled a lot in my young adult years. It caused me a lot of emotional pain and hurt until I had a wake up call that if I did not do something about my dreams, purpose and passion, I would be really sick.

I took a trip to the store and bought paper, paint, brushes and How-to books and I began to paint out the panic, the emotional pain and hurt. With the help of God, I taught myself how to be creative again. I began to paint my dreams.

My dream was to be an artist and write poetry, read books, and teach what I know. In the process of all of this, my emotional state was healed; the panic, anxiety, and depression went out the window because the dream that God had given me became alive in me again.

There is a scripture that says, "We are to stir up the gifts," the dreams that are within us. We have to take steps to make our dreams come true. That is when I knew that it was something about art and being creative that was healing. It aided in my depression; it boosted my mood. I wanted others to be healed also, so I started teaching art as a way to help heal with God's help.

Since then, I had a chance to go to school, college, work in the medical profession taking care of people from all cultures and walks of life. Yes, life is art and I have painted my dream when I applied (painted) what I have learned to my life. And I keep dreaming even if I fail sometimes.

There is a proverb that says that *a righteous man may fall seven times, but will rise and rise again.* Proverbs 24:16.

Think of the picture I painted in the 7th grade of the man in the desert, hot, thirsty, ragged, alone and lost on his journey. I believe his dream kept him alive. So don't give up on life. Life is art, paint your dream.

Malika's Transformation Class
Malika Rahmaan-Davis

This class is to grow me--Get in touch with the person inside. Will the real me (Malika) come forward?

As I was lying in bed last night sleeping, I awoke about 4AM and for the life of me, I couldn't go back to sleep. I knew I had a class this morning. I also knew I was to drive to Gardena Grove, Calif. to pick up my daughter and we were to drive to Carson, Calif. Our very first day of class.

The friend, who had invited me, had promised a **self transformation**. The word **transformation** is very important to me. It says finally I will transform to be the person which almighty God had intended me to be - a woman of virtue -a woman of great character, **transformation**. This class was to be the turning point of my life. I was excited.

I was already attending a class every Saturday that was getting me in touch with "me". Who was I? Why did I think a certain way? What made me act and respond to life situations a certain way? This women's group was certainly a very unique and mind altering class. So this new class could only add to my growth to get to know "me". I am excited!!!! I can't go back to sleep!!!! I toss and turn until 6AM and finally I decide to get up, get dressed, pack a lunch, and get ready to leave.

I am to leave Mo Val at 8AM, drive to Garden Grove, Ca. and arrive in the O.C. at 9AM. This will give me two hours to drive to Carson, CA, where my new class is being held plus an hour to relax, eat snacks and get fresh hot coffee before class begins.

So everything went as planned until we arrived at the freeway off ramp. I wasn't too sure of the exit, so we by passed it, and miles later we realized we were going in the wrong direction. It was another few miles before we could turn around and head back in the right direction. We finally found the right freeway and the right street we should have exited. Now I am frustrated, sweating and irritated with the possibility of being late for a class in which I had started off 2-hours in advance on a thirty minute, 26-mile journey from my daughter's house. Lord, help me!

We still arrived to our destination an hour early, so we headed for the Seven-Eleven store, bought coffee and a hot dog with a free Big Gulp, for only $2.00 dollars. I couldn't bypass this deal. So the food I brought with me from the house, I would keep till later. We then went back to the Center where the class was to be held and we ate our food, drank coffee, and waited.

About an hour later the instructor arrived to let us in. She was a pleasant looking lady and friendly. So the time has finally arrived for me to start the beginning of the "new me".

We went inside and introduced ourselves. She gave us our intro packs and we sat at a table that would hold approx. ten people to sit, talk and discuss things of interest as each person arrived.

The group started slowly with small talk and small jokes, etc. and I was beginning to think I was in the wrong place at this time. I looked in my daughter's direction and I could feel that she was thinking the same thing and feeling the same way I did as her eyes were slightly closed and her bottom lip was protruding out, as it did when she was upset about something.

Then slowly the mood changed and the facilitator took the conversation into a new direction. The woman in front of me started crying and we all turned our attention to her and asked what was the matter? She finally said she had just learned that morning that her four year old was diagnosed with Cerebral Palsy. And she started crying even harder. The lady sitting next to me said what a brave person she was. For many reasons, God had given her the awesome responsibility of taking care of this child, so she was on a learning curve.

She spoke on the many possibilities of blessings she would be acquiring to guarantee her a place in God's Kingdom even though she may not see it in that light as of yet. Some of the ladies there also spoke on the fact that God is in the healing business and to pray and have faith that God has the final word and that it's not over till it's over. And some of us related stories as when the doctors had given people we knew days to live and years later they are still here. Every one around the table including myself shared with her our personal opinions.

The conversation then turned to each of us, one by one. We were asked to say something about ourselves and what brought us here, what did we want or expect to achieve from this class.

So not really knowing just what this class was all about, a couple of people had not shared of themselves. I asked, "Let's hear from them." I was told that in due time, the next meeting. And of course I said to please share a little something such as are you married? Do you have kids, because just the sound of their voices and a little personal tidbit helps to give me a clue into their minds.

Again I was asked to be patient and that my queries also showed I wanted answers quickly. Yea!!!! That's me. What is this class any way? I thought it was going to be a religious class--- go to the Bible chapters and verses type class. Now I am slowly coming to realize that we have a psychiatrist heading this class, and the student sitting next to be appears to be clairvoyant. So this class is beginning to interest me and did I forget to mention that there are at least four Christian ministers in this setting? Hmmm.

Until next week, I will keep you tuned in and let you be the judge of my transformation.

Me and the Egg
Marcia P. Carter-Hill

Preparing food has always been an easy pursuit for Ms. Marci. She is gifted at taking whatever is present and turning it into a very tasty dish. Her fridge and pantry are well stocked at all times. She has quality cookware and loves cooking gadgets. Generally, all goes well, except for the boiling of eggs!

Hard-boiled eggs are used in many ways, including survival, as a convenient protein source. Breakfast, lunch, dinner, snacks, garnishes, and hors d'oeuvre, topped with pimentos, olives, and caviar raise the level of the sophistication of the humble egg.

Accomplishing these healthy delights requires culinary skills that seem to elude me in the kitchen. My dilemma, not the pot, water, or varieties of heat sources all available, ensuring the removal of the shell, as not to damage the appearance of the item is critical!

I have experienced many disappointing results boiling the chicken's gift of eggs, both sizes and colors. No matter what my strategies, if I boiled a dozen, four out of twelve would not be easy to peel! I really like eggs and can't resist reaching for them whether presented plain or fancy. No special event or holiday is necessary.

Over the years, I have done my research pertaining to the execution of the egg boiling task. I can do a lot in a skillet, having rid the item of its shell, even cracking them open with one trained hand like a pro chef. I have conferred with grandmas, caterers, friends, chicken farmers, the Internet, and YouTube for guidelines for defeating the removal of that shell and membrane that holds on dearly to the white and yolk of the treasured egg. Every suggestion is always touted as foolproof.

First, the old fashion way, large pot, tepid water, room temperature eggs not crowded, a stove burner and blue flames beneath; remembering to not boil too vigorously, causing them to bump into each other and crack open. Back then, the chickens were probably the original "free range" birds that pecked at dirt, gravel, live worms, and bugs, while drinking muddy water in the yard. Somehow the eggs had more flavor and were not as obstinate about being peeled. Yes, they were soiled by the natural environment of the nest and needed washing off. Today's modern cooks would be appalled for sure. So, we pay more dearly for red-stamped, high quality, "free range" eggs, properly cleaned.

On with the research. I noted that most of today's eggs, for the supermarkets, are laid by a breed of chicken named, White Leghorns, millions of them working very hard, day and night, to supply the demands of consumers. Poor things. My grandmother had Rhode Island Reds running around her backyard, a few black-speckled hens, and some interestingly creamy-beige hens as well. Those eggs had the deepest colored yolks and clearest whites that I recall. I used to watch her throw out all of the discarded vegetable stems, old bread, dry corn kernels, grains of many descriptions, and something called "mash". I wonder what they are fed nowadays.

Later, shared suggestions were, salt the water used, add vinegar to the water, boil slowly with the pot covered with a lid, and pierce the large end of the egg with a needle, being sure to puncture through the membrane. A cooking instructor swears by gently boiling for fifteen minutes, cover the pot and set aside for ten minutes, pour off water and give eggs an ice bath for five minutes. Now, smack the eggs on the counter top to start the first cracks and gently roll on a paper towel. The shell should be easy to remove. Got it! Does it work? Sometimes, but there's always one that fights you back.

Still later times, a new innovative gadget holds the eggs in a plastic tray, covered by a plastic dome. Place the gadget into a microwave oven for about seven minutes. Note, they are not covered by water, but the water is below the eggs and they are steamed. Imagine the tactic. Believe it or not, I got good results with peeling them, plus they were still warm enough to melt butter.

The latest Saturday morning television promotional places the already boiled egg, cracked on each end, on a plastic platform, and a bellows-type device, like that used to encourage the flames in a fireplace to ignite, is set on top of the unit, and you exert sharp forceful pressure downward and lo and behold the egg pops out. It's recommended practicing to achieve perfection and going to YouTube for visuals. Yes, you can do this. Never a hassle again.

Promise! Only $19.99, free shipping and handling. But wait! Call in the next ten minutes and get an egg slicer along with it. Oh, my goodness. What next?

I will keep investigating, but I am hungry, and in a big hurry, so I grabbed two eggs, cracked them sharply on the side of a bowl, and let the albumen and yolk drop into the bowl. I beat them to death with a whisk. You can add a teaspoon of water or milk to break down the viscosity of the whipped eggs and pour them into a non-stick moderately heated skillet. Once the eggs have congealed on the bottom of the pan, using a bamboo flat-edge spoon or turner, drag the outside edges of the eggs towards the center of the pan. Allow uncooked egg to flow to the outside pan edges and slow the cooking process by lifting the skillet up from the burner grate. Now, using a swirling motion of the pan, finish the eggs to your desired doneness. Do not press down or stir the eggs. Let them just naturally puff up with the internal gases and heated air. Simply slide them out and onto a warm plate, garnish as you like and enjoy!

Minerva On the Express
Anne Hendricks-Jones

Minerva boarded the Amtrak Acela Express, the bullet train, and settled down for a two-hour ride to Baltimore from New York. She was exhausted. Killing takes a lot out of a tired old woman so she pushed the button to recline her seat. It did not do so. After several tries, she gave up and complained to a passing conductor. He informed her that the young man behind her had placed seat defenders on her seat so that it could not recline. Unfortunately, Amtrak did not have a policy on seat defenders, currently, as this was a new development, so he would ask the young man to take them out but if he refused, there was nothing that could be done. He did so and of course, the passenger refused. When she asked if she could have another seat, she was informed that there were no other seats; that the only other option was to get on another train. The conductor walked away.

"Young man. Please remove those seat defender do-hickies from my seat. You can see that I am a tired old lady. My back hurts, my hip hurts, and my feet hurt and I must get some rest."

"Lady," he replied insolently, not even looking up from his laptop. "Your hurting back is not my problem."

"Young man, don't be rude. Didn't your mother teach you to respect your elders?"

Tiredly, he looked up. "YOU are REALLY bothering me. Shut up, leave me alone, and let me do my work!" He went back to typing on his computer.

Minerva stood up. She noticed that the portly man was drinking large amounts of a popular energy drink. There were already four empty cans that she could see, on his adjoining seat table. He would need to go to a restroom very shortly.

She went to the ladies restroom and waited. Sure enough, the man stood up and came down the aisle. As he passed the door to the ladies rest room, she reached out, grabbed him, and pulled him in. While holding him with a half nelson around his neck, Minerva dislodged her derringer from her left sleeve and showed it to him.

"See this, you little snit!" she said, the anger boiling out. "If I place this next to your temple and pull the trigger, your brain will plaster this bathroom wall and you won't need your laptop ever again. I am an assassin, and I and my assassin friends, seated all around you, on this train, don't appreciate rude, inconsiderate assholes like you, taking advantage of little old ladies. I see you have already wet your pants so you don't need the restroom after all. Go back to your seat, pull out those seat defenders, move to my seat, relax, and get off at the next stop, if you want to live. My derringer will be pointed at the back of your head. Don't do anything that would make me put a hole in it. I wouldn't want to inconvenience the passenger in front of you. Do I make myself clear?"

He gave a weak "yes" and she let him go, pointing the gun at his nose. Nothing in all his years of playing computer games had prepared him for this. He walked like a zombie back to his seat, cleaned it, removed the seat defenders, and moved his stuff to her seat. Before sitting, he looked around to see if he could see her buddies, her fellow assassins, but there was really no way to tell, so he sat quietly, frozen in place and did nothing to excite or offend anyone else. He got off at the next stop, weak with relief that she did not follow him. From then on, he would steer clear of little old ladies, reply politely if any chose to address him, and never, ever use the seat defenders again.

Minerva, on the other hand, felt her work was done, set her chair to recline, and went to sleep.

Missing Shoes
Cathy Fortin-Jenkins

The Japanese Bridge in Harrisburg's Italian Lake separates two large sections of the lake. In the summertime, ducks and swans waddle across the stairs of the bridge instead of swimming across the lake.

In the winter, the ducks were sunning themselves in southern climes in the south and who knows where the swans were. I was there in the winter with two carloads of friends to ice skate. Some of us were in high school and some were in the eighth grade at the school in our town. Along the lake were park benches where the girls sat to put on their skates while the boys just plopped on the bank, put on their skates, and were off.

The girls carefully lined up their shoes and boots under the park bench and took note of the location of the bench midway between the eastern edge of the lake and the Japanese Bridge. The girls started out slowly skating around the center of the lake. The ice was crowded with parents teaching their children to skate. Some of the children were barely out of toddler hood. Some folks came prepared for the cold with large thermos bottles filled with hot chocolate, the smell of which wafted onto the ice as we were passing. As the crowd thinned out, the boys became rambunctious and started chasing the slower skating girls. With screams and giggles, the girls skated faster. Then we all joined hands and started a 'crack the whip'. Some older larger boys joined our group adding their muscle to the end of the whip that cracked all the girls at the other end. The girls zoomed practically out of control. They held on with a near death grip.

Exhaustion soon followed after all that skating. It was time to head home; our Sunday night was ending and we glumly thought of school the next day.

The girls headed to their shoes under the park bench where I was to find that my shoes were missing. Exasperated, I thought my toes would be frost-bitten before I got to my friend's car so I walked on the thin skate blades over clumps of frozen mud and patches of ice looking for my shoes. The girls went around the bench in all directions searching for any glimpse of my old, dirty white bucks that had seen better days. They were ugly but I wanted my shoes. At that point, I was almost crying when one of the boys who apparently had a crush on me, picked me up and threw me over his shoulder and proceeded to jostle me around laughing heartedly. I was indignantly shouting, "Put me down!" Everyone was laughing as my captor headed for the parking lot carrying me without my shoes.

My knight in shining armor minus his white horse came to my rescue. He was bigger and smarter than the caveman carrying me. Also, my knight was the driver of the car. He simply said, "Get her shoes!"

So, Chas, the caveman, carried me, still upside down and squealing to the side of the Japanese Bridge that was painted red amidst the white and gray of winter. The caveman had hidden my shoes behind a pile of snow by the bridge. He not so gently deposited me on a pile of snow. Switching from caveman style, Chas became gallant and helped me unlace my skates. He waited patiently for me to put on my old comfy though icy shoes. Then off we went to face school the next day and the wintry looking nuns clad in black and white.

My Dad
Jain Householder

He was not mine when first we met
His eyes, nose and mouth were all different
from mine, and yet,
He was now my Dad.

My mom and I trudged through
10 years of life without a man in our home,
without a dad for a daughter.
I was 15 when this person called a "step" came
into my life.

What is a stepfather to someone with no
expectations?
He stepped forward and said, "I'll take her to
be my child."
He stepped out of his comfort zone to take on
the responsibility of yet another child.
He stepped back in his spending on his own
children to support someone else's.

He stepped into my life and gave me
encouragement and guidance.
He stepped up to defend me when I needed
defending.
He stepped lightly when he knew I was
hurting.
He stepped next to me at the front of the line

when it came time to walk me down the aisle
and hand me over to the next man in my life.

He was not mine when first we met,
His eyes, nose and mouth were different from
mine, and yet,
He was my Dad.

My Doll with the Broken Leg
Emma Fay Jones

There was great excitement the evening before the trip. My sisters and I was helping Mama pack our suitcases. Our ages were five, six and seven.

Mama was packing things we needed and we were packing things we wanted, but Mama would come right behind us, taking things out we didn't need, like my doll with the broken leg. I wanted to take her with me because I loved my doll. I had broke her leg putting her in an old trunk. The lid slipped out of my hand and came down hard on her leg. I felt so bad; it was as if my own leg had broke. My daddy had said he would fix the leg but never got around to it.

Mama tossed the doll in the chair. I wanted to take my doll with me. I had gotten her for Christmas but it was two weeks after Christmas that I received her. When I had awakened Christmas morning there was no doll under the tree only a big red wagon with lots of fruits and nuts. I wanted a doll so bad. I went to Mama and Daddy and asked, "All I wanted was a doll. Why didn't Santa leave me a doll?" They gave me an excuse about me awaking in the night and it must have scared Santa before he could leave the doll.

About two weeks later, I heard my mother calling me. "Fay, Fay." I went running into her room. She reached up and put her hands down beside the bed and up she came with this doll. It was the most beautiful doll I had ever seen. Her dress was blue with yellow and red pink flowers and a bonnet to match with white socks and shoes. "Santa left this for you," she said. "You must have awakened Christmas night and Santa heard you and left so quick he forgot to put your doll under the tree." I was so excited and happy that I now had a doll. But now we were leaving her and I had to figure out something.

The evening went by fast, packing, bathing, and getting our hair done. We were busy.

We were going to live with our daddy who had left to find a job in another state. Mama was so happy. I could hardly sleep that night. The night was so long. I just lay there listening to the crickets and frogs and the old owl hooting and thought about my doll with the broken leg.

We were up before dawn. I had not slept too well and I could hear my mother up stirring around in the kitchen making fire in the old iron stove. The smell of the wood burning and the aroma of biscuits and fried chicken filled my nostrils. We washed and ate breakfast. I watched as Mama packed our lunches for the trip wrapping biscuits, chicken and even pound cake in pieces of feed sack that had been washed and then bleached by the sun. Who was going to eat all that food? I knew I could not eat another bite. Soon we were all dressed, packed and ready to go.

My sisters and I were all dressed in our white dresses and white slips, socks and black shoes. Our hair had been pressed with the hot comb and braided with white ribbons into the braids all down to the end and tied into a big bow.

We arrived at the train station excited. Mama was

busy checking things in her purse. The train arrived at the station with whistles blowing steam and smoke and rails screeching. We watched as it came to a slow grinding stop. Out came this man all in black with a cap with a white band around it. Mama told us to follow her and we did, carrying our suitcases. Mama gave the man the tickets. He told us where to go. We all sat in the back of the train. I got a seat by the window. The train pulled off and we were on our way.

It seemed like two or three days we were on the train. Every now and then we would stop and eat biscuits, chicken and cake. Mama would change our dresses every day and comb our hair and tell us not to get dirty.

At night on the train after everyone settled down and there was nothing left to look at out the window, I would close my eyes and think about my doll with the broken leg tucked deep down in my suitcase. I had got her out of the chair where Mama had tossed it. I knew that when the trip was over and I saw my daddy, he would fix it.

My Rainbow of Hugs
Pamela Cockerham

If I could hold or catch a rainbow I would do it
just for you. And I would share with you its
beauty.

If I could build a mountain out of a grain of
sand for you to call your own, you would have
a palace to find serenity, a place to be alone.

If I could take all of your troubles, hurts, pain
and toss them in the sea, I would,
But I'm finding all these things
are too impossible for me.

Well, I cannot build a mountain,
hold or catch a rainbow anywhere
Just let me be what I am best - a friend that is
always there!

My Secret Closet

Pamela Cockerham

There is a certain place in my house
That no one knows about,
Where I can go to Jesus,
And pour my guts out.

It isn't a very large space
It doesn't need to be,
Just big enough for the two of us
My Savior God and me.

When I go into my closet
I shut out everything,
I need the peace and quiet
That solitude can bring.

I clear my heart of any malice
And all that is not clean
I call upon the master
And on his arms I lean.

New Revelations
Marge Ramsey

At the end of my granddaughter Cori's eighth grade year, I had an opportunity to take her to a week long softball tournament in Colorado. Normally her parents would accompany us, but her sister Abby had a tournament coming up in Utah. Time and finances did not permit her family to attend both.

I was very excited about this trip. On our flight to Colorado, Cori met the mother of a girl on another team, and found that she knew a couple of the girls on Cori's team. The whole team stayed in the same hotel so we spent a lot of time with them, which gave me an opportunity to get to know the parents better.

As we were getting ready for bed the first night, Cori asked me to remind her in the morning to take her hair ribbon. I suggested she put it with my purse, and her response was simply, "I can't." The next morning we had breakfast at the hotel before heading out to the softball field. Cori, being a catcher, had a very large bag that sported her bats, gloves and catcher's gear. Thank goodness it had wheels. As we were walking out the door, she suddenly dropped the handle of her bag and it went crashing to the floor. She turned back into the room and straightened both her shoes and mine, then said, "Ok, we can go now."

Back in the hotel room that evening I realized that her hair brush, bobby pins and toothbrush were very neatly aligned on the counter. Our shoes stood proudly in a very straight row.

Thinking back, I remembered mentioning to her mom that Cori was doing some very strange things. There would be notes around the house that said things like "put on deodorant," "brush teeth," "brush hair." These are things that most people do automatically without thinking about them. Why would you need written reminders? This was my first real awareness of the fact that she had OCD, obsessive-compulsive disorder.

Cori was struggling in school and was barely maintaining a C average. Part of the problem was forgetting to take homework to school after taking the time to actually do it. She was also doing poorly on tests, partly because she never finished them. The whole thing about writing notes and struggling in school finally prompted her mom to take her to a counselor who was recommended through the assistance program at work. His diagnosis was ADHD, OCD and insomnia. She was referred to psychiatrist for further evaluation and medication if she deemed necessary.

I will skip ahead a few years to share with you what she wrote in her college admission essay.

"In my freshman year I thought that I was not extremely smart, more of an average student. I did not believe in myself much. I was conservative because I did not want to look for a reason to speak out. Once I was medicated, I gradually began to realize my intelligence, thought processes, creativity, ability to learn quickly, and much more. I found that my distractibility and inability to do all of my work had to do with my ADHD, Attention Deficit Hyperactivity Disorder, and OCD. By the second semester of sophomore year, I was answering questions in class, participating in debates, expressing my creative ideas, and helping others to learn new lessons, all while astounding everyone around me. I found that I actually learned and remembered better by using colored pens. I learned that doing my class notes, homework, and all other assignments in pen helped it all stick in my head. I found that I did better in smaller and one-on-one settings and that I did better with visuals and explanations."

"I have grown as a person by having to learn how to work with my disabilities. Some might say that what I have can keep me from doing well and can put me at a disadvantage. I strongly disagree. Although it may be harder for me to do what I want, I have no reason to believe that I will not be able to do it. As for 'being at a disadvantage,' I think that I actually have an advantage rather than a disadvantage. My disabilities have helped me to get to know myself extremely well, made me work more than twice as hard, and come up with strategies to help me from day to day. I now know that I have always been intelligent, innovative, creative, and much more. I might stumble, or even fall sometimes, but it is not about how many times you get knocked down, it is about how many times you get back up."

Cori has gone from struggling in her freshman year of high school to completing her second year of college at Ottawa University in Kansas. She made the

Dean's List while also playing catcher all season during her freshman and sophomore years for the varsity softball team. She has discovered a new passion for history, and is already talking about getting her master's degree. I applaud this young lady's accomplishments and see her through admiring eyes. Not just as my granddaughter, but as someone who will take the working world by storm, quietly, and stand above her disabilities.

Note on the Windshield
Mona Lisa Stallworth

I cannot believe I forgot about Daylight Saving Time! How could I have gone all day without realizing it and now it's Monday morning and I am late getting up for my major presentation. Now this is just great! I thought. What else could go wrong on this big day? Well, I did not have to wait long to find out because as I was putting on my hosiery, I poked a giant hole right in the middle of my left pantyhose leg! And of course it was my last pair!!!

Now, I had to hurry and rummage around to find a suitable pant suit to wear: no, bare legs would not be appropriate for this presentation. Then, I remembered I had picked up my cleaning on Saturday. Immediately I rushed to locate the suit and assemble the correct accessories to match my new attire.

Finally, I headed for the door only to realize I didn't have my keys. I always keep them on the peacock key holder near the door. I don't believe this! Where did I put them? I thought. Then I proceeded to spend the next few minutes searching everywhere only to discover them in my jacket pocket. I had accidentally brought them upstairs Saturday with the cleaning. When I saw them, while getting the pantsuit, I immediately put them in the jacket pocket so that I would have them when I got ready to leave; smart idea, right? But then I forgot I had done it! What a morning!

Alright, I can still make it on time, I thought to myself, if there is no traffic. That thought too was short lived. As soon as I entered onto the freeway on ramp all I could see for miles were red brake lights staring back at me! No one was moving. Wonderful, I thought.

As the traffic slowly began to move, I saw the source of the delay. There was a major accident involving many cars. I could tell that it had not been long since the accident occurred since there were no emergency vehicles or highway patrol cars on the scene yet.

I began to think, 'Wow! maybe if I had not had all those delays, maybe I would have been involved in that pile up.' I began to be thankful and although I was late, I arrived with a smile on my face. I got out of my car feeling very blessed and I even had a little pep in my step.

The meeting actually went very well; however, when I returned to my car I could see someone had placed a note on my windshield. Oh! No! I thought. Did someone hit my car? Was this some kind of a ticket?

I slowly approached my car and began to examine it for signs of an accident. I checked the rear and both sides, but I saw no signs of any damage. I looked at the overhead signs to see if maybe by mistake I had parked in a reserve place, but no, it said 'visitor'. I then proceeded with caution to remove the note from my windshield.

I opened the note and started reading it. Immediately I began to weep. It was from a man. He said he had a horrible morning and was very distraught; in addition, he had recently lost his wife. She was a very happy person and was positive about everything. She could find the silver lining in every situation no matter how bad it appeared. He went on to say, he sure needed her that day.

Then he saw me. I had such a smile on my face and I walked with a kind of joy and peace that reminded him of his wife. He thanked me for reminding him of her and what she would have said to him. He felt I was a sign from her to stay positive and remember that this too shall pass!

I stood there thinking: what if I had not changed my attitude about all that had occurred before I arrived for my presentation? What if he had seen frustration? What if I had been wearing a frown? What if I had walked slowly with my head down like the weight of the world was on my shoulders? Or like I had just been beaten by life?

I will always cherish that note as a reminder of how my attitude, disposition and mannerism may affect others around me. You never know who's watching you!

Once Upon A Sleeper
Clyde Schweitzer

The ejected casing skipped across the cold tile bathroom floor as the 100-grain projectile slipped from the silencer deep into John's frontal lobe. His body crumpled to the floor like a discarded bath towel.

My hand shook as I withdrew my extended arm and placed the 9-millimeter Glock in its hiding place beneath my jacket. I had killed many a men and regrettably two women. Some face to face, eyeball to eyeball, but never one I knew personally. Not until now. I couldn't believe the person he sent was John.

After our third raiding party was ambushed there was a growing suspicion that a traitor was hiding among us. In a secret meeting early this morning the Captain revealed his suspicions to me. My instruction was to eliminate whoever showed up at this abandoned motel.

I took a deep breath and gritted my teeth. As the Captain said, "If the cell was to survive security must prevail at all cost."

Once again I peered down at John's body then up at the door. I'll have to mind my step to avoid the slowly evolving blood pool, I thought. I shook my head. Poor dumb SOB. What made the Captain suspect him? It didn't make any sense.

That question continued to fester as I approached the broken bathroom window. Balancing on my tiptoes, I placed my fingertips on the window ledge and peered out. Through the ebbing heat of the dusty twilight I surveyed the remnants of what was once a thriving little oasis on State 23 that had been turned into an instant ghost town once the motorway was finished. The evening breeze chased a tumbleweed through the empty bay of the abandoned Texaco gas station then across the crumbling asphalt out into the sweeping never, never.

Finally reliving the tension in my calves, I stepped back, turned and retreated towards the door. Negotiating my way around the coagulating pool of blood I continued through the bedroom and out into the parking lot. I checked my watch, then the empty pavement all the way to the horizon.

Where the hell are you Philip? I mumbled to myself.

I leaned up against a crumbling brick wall that once outlined a small patio and lit a cigarette. As I waited I found myself staring into the vastness of the star lit night sky pondering the circumstance that brought me to this God forsaken place.

It had only been a few months after the elections when the "New Society" started clamping down personal freedoms. Some of the opposition suddenly disappeared overnight. Any voice against the new government was quickly silenced. But that's what happens when people become too complacent with their government.

As long as their own little corner of the world isn't threatened and they allow twenty percent of the population to rule the other eighty, the dark side of humanity will eventually creep in and engulf everything. History will and does repeat itself. It happened in Italy and Germany in the 1930s. And in Cambodia and Burma in the seventies.

Now that it has happened here the only means for the masses to regain control is by force. The time finally came when everyone had to pick a side.

John and I stepped forward that first night. I knew my wife would have a fit so I waited to tell her until one of her favorite television commentators suddenly disappeared.

Ah,

Finally a glimmer of light crept over the horizon. I squatted behind the wall and readied my gun. As the jeep skidded to a stop the dust it had created quickly caught up and engulfed the headlights.

An instant later a figure all dressed in black appeared from the far side grimacing, blinking and waving his hands back and forth as if he could part the dust before him.

I rose from my hiding as Philip approached. "Is the dirty deed done?"

"Yes, yes it's done. But tell me this. How did you get the Captain to believe it was John?"

"Well, you did tell me he was as dumb as dirt."

"Yes, that's why I nominated him."

"Why do you think he picked me for this job?"

"What I want to know is what tipped the scales in John's direction? He was as straight as an arrow."

Philip grinned. "It must have been that receipt for his little girl's doll I dug out of his trash."

I shook my head. "You are an evil bastard."

"Well, the last time we met you did say your Captain was getting suspicious." Then he smiled, "Better him than you, right?"

I nodded.

"Now that this cell is all but eliminated the Counsel wants you to move over to Newtown. You'll find there has been a sudden opening for a third grade teacher at Sunny Vail Elementary."

Reaching into his back pocket he extracted my payment. "With your reputation you'll have no problem fitting right in."

I took the envelope and nodded back over my shoulder. "What about John; aren't we going to bury him?

"Nah, grounds too hard."

As Philip disappeared around the far side of the jeep I shouted, "What about the police?"

"You forget, I am the police," came his answer from the darkness.

Pier Pressure

James Otis Harris

Corey looked over the animals that have lined up in his courtroom. It was time to begin. Corey slammed his magic spoon on the milk crate and it began to sing.

"Bring your problems to Judge Corey no matter the size. Welcome to Corey's courtroom. Will everyone please rise!"

The animals stood as his song echoed around the barn. Corey was curious as to whom he was seeing today. Bailiff Ben told Corey, "The goose family, Mr. and Mrs. Waddle are here with their son Henry."

Corey called in the family.

Mr. and Mrs. Waddle rocked from side to side as they entered the courtroom. Mr. Waddle wore a long lavender tie with white polka dots that hung from his neck. Mrs. Waddle wore a straw hat with purple and pink flowers on it. The Waddle family had always been nice. Their children were never in trouble. Corey wondered why they were here.

Corey asked, Mr. and Mrs. Waddle "What brings you into my court today?"

Mr. Waddle spoke first. "Good morning, Judge Corey," he said with a quack. His broad smile stretched across his face. "Over the last few weeks the missus and I have noticed Henry acting funny. He began hanging around kids called the Gliders. They are named the Gliders because when they swim, they glide real smooth across the lake. They are known to be trouble on the barnyard.

"Yesterday, I saw Henry and the Gliders standing on the edge of the pier. They were going to dive into the lake. This is usually no big deal, but in the late afternoon, it can be dangerous. You see, you can't see the huge black rocks from the pier after 4:00. Since kids have been hurt diving off the pier, Sheriff Croc posted no diving signs after 4:00 around the lake.

"We told Henry about diving off the pier with his new friends. He just folded his arms and frowned his face. He uttered under his breath, 'I guess I'll never have any friends,' and ran to his room. Two days later we received a call from Dr. Doogie telling us Henry had broken his arm from jumping off the pier! He doesn't think he did anything wrong. So we brought Henry to see you today."

Corey remembered the Gliders. They had been in his courtroom two days earlier for jumping off the pier. Corey stared at Henry. Henry felt his stomach hurt like the time he ate three mouthfuls of candy real fast. Corey asked, "What do you have to say about this?"

Henry had always been undersized for a goose. His neck was short, his wings small, and his beak was tiny. He often wondered when he would grow.

"Well, your honor, I like the Gliders. They're cool! I know they're a few years older than me but they let me hang around with them. My old barnyard pals are boring. The Gliders aren't so bad, Judge Corey. You just don't know them."

Corey asked, "How did you hurt your arm?"

"I was standing on the pier with the Gliders and

was told if I wanted to hang with the big Gliders, I would have to pass a test. The guys said I had to jump into Lake Whatcadoing at 4:30 in the afternoon. This was my chance to be one of the guys.

"I told them what my parents said about diving in the lake at dark. The leader of the Gliders said, 'Do you always do what your parents say? Those no diving signs are for those who are scared. If you want to be a part of us you have to jump or go home'

"I wanted to be part of the Gliders so I jumped. When 1 looked down I didn't see any rocks, but soon after I hit the water I felt my arm hurting. The guys just ran away when they saw I was hurt. Some of my old friends from class helped me out of the water and took me to the hospital. Doc Doggie told me I had broken my arm."

Corey glanced around the courtroom before looking at Henry. "This sounds like a case of Peer Pressure," he said.

Corey opened his Barnyard Book of Rules and asked, "What is Peer Pressure?" The book hopped around the desk and stopped in front of Corey. It opened to the orange page with the fancy white "P" in the corner. It speaks.

"When Peer Pressure is the test, don't follow the rest. When it's all said and done, a true friend won't run."

Corey leaned forward and said, "Henry, you should listen to your parents. Peer pressure from the Gliders caused you to jump off the pier and break your arm. Your true friends are the ones who helped you to the hospital, not the ones who ran."

"I rule this is a case of Peer Pressure and Henry, you must tell your parents you are sorry for not listening to them."

Henry turned to his parents with his broken arm in a green and red sling and told them he was sorry for not listening. The family hugged and waddled out of the barn.

Corey faced the animals and said, "The moral of this case is, your friends are the ones who help you out of trouble, not the ones who help you find it."

Corey stood up, slammed his wooden spoon down on the milk crate and said, "Court is adjourned. See you tomorrow!"

Power to Change:
A Pivotal Life Decision
Marcia Carter-Hill

What would you change if you could?

It is now the tenth day that I have struggled with this thought-provoking topic. I sat on my deck one morning, while living in Bardstown, Kentucky, trying to envision myself as one of the trees behind my house. There are some that grow straight up, not bushy, cylindrical in shape. I paid particular attention to that tree thinking of myself, taller than other kids during my childhood. During my youth, and being female in the fifties, I towered over my friends and my teachers! It was always an uncomfortable feeling. I was teased, often being called string bean, scarecrow, and long legs. I had recurring dreams of a surgeon cutting out about two inches or more at my ankles, making me more equal to other girls my age. Ballet slippers were my best choice of footwear followed by Mary Jane flats. Over time, I learned to live with my height, as it certainly was not anything I could change. I even wore three-inch heels as an adult.

Still studying those trees, I decided that the trunk was like a person's core and the large branches the diversions on their walk through life. The twigs represent the vast experiences, some shorter and weaker, breaking off easily. If I were measuring the distance of the protrusions on that branch, it might represent a time line of my walk during life.

One nice healthy branch had twigs of career choices. My early choices were singer, secretary, stenographer and dancer, like my mother whom I never recall actually living with on a daily basis. Later, my goals and desires were wife and mother, secretary, schoolteacher, nurse, and writer. I have done all of these things a little. Outside of motherhood, my changes would have been to hone in on my God-given talents with more intensity than I have, attending college and getting a degree in the medical field or engineering. I love surgical shows and I invent things that I need to use in my hobbies and work.

A long twig to the right had many little stems, some longer and some broken off. I related that to the romances throughout my journey that are all gone at this time, as I live a single life, happily! Looking back now, that branch would have possibly been better for me without those broken stems that complicated my walk.

I often say, "If I knew then, what I know now, my choices would have been very different." The statement might not be true, because I don't think that you can live your life without making choices based on conditions at the time. You haven't ever been at that point in your life before and no matter what parents, friends, clergy or anyone else advise you, we must be ourselves and tread the path alone to our destiny. Maybe our paths are predestined at birth and we stagger along wondering how and why we are motivated to do what we do.

At this point in my life, I have decided that it is futile to ponder over what might have been, because it is more important to speculate on what future choices I can make based on past years of experiences.

Putting it all together, I can travel each step of life one at a time, choosing right or left, always moving forward until the road closes. I might not change anything, for I've been blessed in many ways and so much more than many others.

Your blessings come every moment with each breath that you take, every movement you make, and seeing all that is around you. Enjoy the sky, the sunrays, clouds, wind and rain, heat and cold, and be thankful for family, neighbors, and close friends. Enjoy and nurture pets and wildlife. Give of yourself to those less fortunate. Be cheerful and smile sending out joyful sounds of laughter.

Be grateful for your life.

Right or Wrong?
Karen (Kay) Donner

Some would say that I am vicious and that I have an insatiable hunger and thirst. Um, some might be right. I have been known to wreak havoc on many innocent people. As Zeus explained to Prometheus, I would not be good for people. Was he right? Or was he wrong?

Some might be tolerant, even tender in their opinion of me. I have been invited into homes of the rich and the poor, the powerful and the incapable, the sick and the healthy. I am, at least and again at most, a beguiling and awesome phenomenon. I have no boundaries and entertain no prejudices.

Today you will join me on a journey that many before traveled. Beware. The hour is approaching. The sun is about to set. The stars will shine tonight and the moon will shimmer like a phosphorescent orb. The weather is perfect. A gentle breeze stirs the air. Summer is here. People are out to play. I stand by, eager and ready to display my attributes.

Let us begin at the ocean's shoreline; there, by a group of young people, see my light, feel my warmth. Oh, how many times I have heard these songs sung around me, *'Cum-Ba-Ya, My Lord'* and *'Ninety-nine Bottles of Beer on the Wall.'* You remember don't you? "Ahh", you say, "those were the days."

The hot dogs roasting on the ends of wire coat hangers filling the air with a mouth watering aroma.

Look at those teen-agers snuggling into each other as my magic fills their minds with thoughts of love. Yes, my presence has often sparked the flame of romance in the hearts of many, but sad, isn't it, how you tend to forget that sense of tranquility, valor, or perhaps fearlessness you had as you gazed upon me one night long ago at a 'beach party'?

Let us journey from the coast and find our way to the forested area we know as a campground. Look now at that family sitting with their small children around a popping, brilliant, blaze. They've eaten their little toasted, sugary, globs they call marshmallows. Their eyes are glued to me in a mesmerizing state. Daddy has explained that they are safe from any of the woodland creatures found in this area because *I* will keep them safe. Daddy then continues to tell them the story of the Monster who hides in the woods. The Monster that only appears when there is a full moon just as there is tonight. The children are enraptured but they know they are safe because of me! They look to me for comfort and for security. They begin to grow weary and fall asleep, just as Daddy had planned. Mom and Dad continue to relax and enjoy the spectacle before them. They see a bit of life from me carried away in a glowing ember and watch it as if they might someday have the ability to fly off in some such fashion. They know that one small piece of me could begin an uncontrolled rage that would kill. Ah, good, they carefully douse me before leaving for the evening. However, they will not soon lose the radiance they received from me this night. The memories made tonight may last a lifetime.

You are growing weary, and so we shall quickly travel through other territories.

A snow covered land. Having me here is a necessity. Nothing else brings more pleasure than viewing me and having me in captivity. I am, in many ways, a God-sent lifesaver.

On a battlefield where cold, hungry service men and women are forlorn, lonesome, and hurting. I can lift spirits. I am a sight that gives peace, hope, heat, and food.

Here, in the sanctity of a home, especially towards the Christmas season, I am seen as a sign of a wonderful gift. Children may think of Santa, adults may think of Christ, others may simply think of relaxation, but in a home, I bring a personal sense of happiness and rest.

So, you see. I am beguiling and a bit hypnotic. I have no prejudices. Most of you love me and welcome me. But, beware, for I am also vicious. I wreak havoc. I have an insatiable appetite and thirst. I know no boundaries. Prometheus knew you could not live any better than the beast if you did not have me, fire. Zeus knew you would become careless. Was Zeus right, or was he wrong?

Stay warm. Eat well. Be happy. Beware.

Shady People

Pamela Cockerham

Why Can't You Accept People For Who They Are?
Grass Can't Provide You Shade

While Starla (who is a friend of mine) and I were walking beside the beautiful stream, we gazed at the tall green grass on the side of the streams of water. As we walked, we looked up at the tall trees with huge leaves. The different shapes and sizes of the leaves were so amazing.

Starla asked me a question, "Why can't people stop talking bad about each other and stop breaking each other's hearts? They need to change and be different," said Starla.

She started off talking about incidents that had happened in her life, which was fine, until it turned into something different. It became complaining about one thing after another.

She literally had a throng of complaints. As we continued on our walk, she began complaining about the heat and other things. We walked and walked, "It's too hot," she said, "Let's walk over there next to the tree, I don't want to be in the heat."

She was very uncomfortable, so I said, "Starla, look at this grass. What do you think of it?"

"It's green, it's nice. But it's hot over here."

"Ask me what I think of this grass? It's pretty and green," I said to Starla, in order to appreciate the grass you had to stand in direct sunlight.

So Starla and I walked in the grass. She admitted it was different, kind of unusual.

"Wow! I love this grass. It is beautiful. But it is hot out here. Let's stand under the beautiful trees right over there."

She started walking ahead of me.

I said, "No, Let's stand and admire the grass and cool off."

"We can't cool off in this grass, okay."

But you just said the grass was beautiful and green."

Starla said, "Yes I did."

I said, "Okay. So let's stay here."

"It is hot, I can't get cool in this grass standing here."

So we walked to the big tree that gave shade and sat down and continued talking. I said, "Starla, why did you get mad at the grass when it couldn't provide you the shade you wanted?"

She looked really confused.

So I put it to her this way, "People are the way they are whether they were created that way or because of life's circumstances.

"They are who they are. Stop wishing they were someone else. The next time you get upset with someone because they are the way they are, or not who you think they should be conformed to what you want. Remember the grass. Never get mad at a blade of grass because it's not a tree. Appreciate the grass for what is. Let it provide for you what it can. But don't expect more. Your life will be so much easier when you start letting people be who they are.

And stop expecting them to give you something they don't have or don't know how to give. Just like the grass couldn't provide shade, and that's because it wasn't meant to.

Some people aren't made to give you what you're asking for. So stop looking for it. You will be surprised how much peace you will have when you stand under this tree.

And furthermore, you wouldn't be so upset and get your dandruff up and your underwear in a bunch with people who are like the grass if you had more people who are like trees in your life."

She's Off the Radar Screen
Virginia Faulkner

No need to wear high heels that cause her
feet to ache
Those six-inch platforms are only good to
look at, for goodness sake!
If she were younger and in the game,
She'd probably try to look cute and
endure the pain
No push-up bras or tight fitting clothes
No need to attract male attention or
envious female foes
She doesn't have to smile seductively, or
speak in honeyed tones
Lower her eyelids or worry about going
home alone
She's invisible to the roving eye
And can easily let sleeping dogs lie
She's off the radar screen.

Her smile comes naturally and when it
does it's real
To wear makeup or not, it's her choice
what to conceal
She can expand her waist with good food
or not
To lose or gain weight is a health issue,
not an attempt to look hot.

She cooks when she wants to and eats
when and what she pleases
She can talk about movies she's seen,
books she's read or discuss intricate
theses.

She can gaze appreciatively at sunsets
or watch the moon rise
And enjoy nature and consider life's
ebbing and flowing tides
No need to hold her peace, it becomes
easier over time
To wait, watch and savor the sublime
She's off the radar screen.

Taking Someone's Test
is not for the Best
James O. Harris

Today was Corey's birthday. His father promised to take him to get his favorite ice cream, double chocolate fudge. Corey heard a lot of cases today and was starting to get hungry.

When Corey picked up his spoon, it began to sing.

"Bring your problems to Judge Corey, no matter the size. Welcome to Corey's courtroom, will everyone please rise."

"Bailiff Ben, who are we seeing today?"

"Mr. Billy Goatee, the 2nd grade history teacher."

Corey has known him for years. He's a large, tall goat with round glasses sitting on the edge of his nose. They look like they are about to fall off when he bends forward. His long, white beard matches the few white strains of hair on top of his baldhead. A piece of straw hangs from his mouth when he speaks. Corey knew he was a good teacher.

"Good morning, Mr. Goatee. How can I help you today?"

"Your honor, yesterday's test assignment was to write, in your own words, the history of the barnyard and turn it in today. Well, Penny Fox and Sheldon Pony turned in their papers. As I was grading, I noticed Penny's and Sheldon's papers were written in the same handwriting. You see, Penny uses big loops and Sheldon uses little loops with his hoof.

"Both papers had big loops. I asked Penny if she wrote Sheldon's paper and she said yes. I brought Penny and Sheldon to see you about this."

Corey could barely see Penny's face above the desk. She was standing with her hands folded in front of him. Penny was such a small, cute little girl fox. She wore blue overalls with a yellow flower on the chest pocket. Her overalls stopped at her knees where her pink and yellow striped socks began. Her red hair was in two ponytails split right down the middle. Her blue eyes were wide open when Corey asked why she wrote Sheldon's paper for him.

"Well, Judge Corey, Sheldon is wonderful! He is so handsome with his long black mane of hair and his shiny white teeth. He is so strong and fast and everyone in the barnyard loves him. I even have a picture of him hanging in my locker with hearts around it.

"Today is the biggest race of the year against the other barnyards. Sheldon is our hero. He asked me to help him win the big race tomorrow. I asked how. I would do anything to help the barnyard win. He said since he needed to rest for the big race and he didn't have time to write the paper, he asked me if I could write it for him this one time so he could rest.

I didn't think one time would hurt. After all, it was for the benefit of the barnyard. When Mr. Goatee found out, he gave us both bad grades and told us to re-write our papers. Mr. Goatee is making a big deal out of nothing."

Corey asked Sheldon to step forward. Sheldon was the best runner in the barnyard and a little cocky.

Sheldon was wearing his blue and yellow school uniform for the race. Sheldon's legs were short for a pony, but he could outrun the best. That may be because his stomach was so close to the ground. Sheldon stepped forward with his head down looking up at Corey.

"Did you have Penny write your paper so you could run in the big race?"

"Correction, your honor, so I could win the big race," he started to laugh. Corey didn't find that funny.

"Your honor, for years we have lost the race to the other barnyards. This was finally our chance to win! There's nobody faster than me. Mr. Goatee is always giving us homework a day before a race. He could have made an exception this once. Because I had to re-write my paper this morning, I missed the race and we lost again. I hope Mr. Goatee is happy."

Corey asked the bailiff to hand him his Barnyard Book of Rules (Corey uses this book to help him decide who should say I'm sorry)

Corey says, "This sounds like a case of 'Cheating to rest to be the best'." The book begins to rise like a cake and then shrinks back to its normal size. It opens to the light green and orange page with a few little t's in the comer. The book begins to rhyme.

Taking someone's test will not make them the best. To achieve any feat, you must not cheat.

Corey asked Penny to step forward. Penny started to feel sad. She said, "Your Honor, I wasn't trying to do anything wrong. All 1 wanted to do was help us win."

Corey smiled at Penny. "What you did was wrong

when you wrote Sheldon's paper. You should never do someone else's work. Even if it means you may lose a race." Sheldon was hoping Corey wouldn't call him, but he did.

"Sheldon, step forward. Winning a race is not worth cheating on a test or asking someone to help you cheat. I'm disappointed in you."

"Judge Corey, I shouldn't have asked Penny to write my paper."

Corey said, "Therefore I rule that Penny and Sheldon must say I'm sorry to Mr. Goatee for cheating."

Penny and Sheldon turned to Mr. Goatee who was sitting in the audience next to the other animals.

"We're sorry for cheating, Mr. Goatee." Penny hopped on Sheldon's back and they galloped around the courtroom saying, "Next year, we're going to win the big race," and left the courtroom.

Corey said, "The moral of this case is: you should never cheat to win."

Now it was time for his birthday and ice cream. Corey banged his spoon on the table and it said, "Court is adjourned! See you tomorrow."

The Appointment
Anne Hendricks-Jones

You open your eyes and slowly move your groggy head towards the clock on the left end table. It says 07:00 AM. You straighten your neck and try to remember what day it is. Tuesday. You have an appointment at 10:00 AM so you check to see if all systems are go. Feet…moving without pain, check. Knees…some pain. Must remember to take two Tylenol. Check. Back…Oh God, much pain. Change that to two Ibuprofen. Check.

Now it's time to make the whole body sit up in bed. It takes some time. You have to position your body just right and push up with both arms. Up you go with your back screeching all the way and shoulder joints not pleased either.

Your feet finally touch the floor and after waiting for the world to stop twirling, you try standing up to see what your feet or legs have to say about it. Your feet are the most vociferous. They don't appreciate you putting your 100 lbs. on them so early in the morning, but as you start hobbling towards the bathroom, they eventually shut up and allow you to complete your walk in peace.

Morning ablutions complete, you pad into the kitchen for a cup of coffee and to check the TV morning news. The coffee is fantastic but the news not so much. A world leader has been shot and killed and there is an international manhunt for the killer.

"Tsk, tsk," you say to yourself as you head back to the bedroom to get dressed.

As behooves your seventy-seven years, you pick a lovely silk blouse that has ties at the collar for a bow in the front, and a long, ankle-length gabardine skirt in gray. You put on the darling pearl necklace and earrings your late husband gave you and comfortable dark gray shoes which have heels of about one inch. More than that and the neuromas in both balls of the feet will send out pain signals that would put you in a very, very bad mood and have you limping by the end of the day.

As you comb your shoulder-length grey hair into a top knot, you hum along with a classic rock song, playing on the radio, about a hit man, who's available at any price. You smile at the reference, re-check you smartphone for the location of your appointment. The ibuprofen has taken effect and loosened up things nicely so your fingers are no longer stiff. You grab you large, leather tote, and lock the door behind you, BUT, you unlock the door and go back in. Once again, you've neglected to take your blood pressure meds and vitamins. You sigh and shake your head at this the vagrancies of age, take the pills and exit your apartment once more.

Half a dozen people are waiting at the elevator, in the building across from your appointment, but they all step aside to allow you to enter first, one of the rare perks of being elderly and somewhat hunched over, you guess. One gentleman even asks if he can help with your bag but you tell him no, with your most genteel smile and he backs off, satisfied he has done his good deed for the day. All of your fellow passengers are gone by the time you reach your destination, the 35th floor. "End of the line," you say to yourself and exit out onto the roof of the office building.

Outside, it is a beautiful summer day, with glorious fresh air and a gentle breeze that loosens a few strands of your hair and makes you so very thankful to be alive, in spite of your aches and pains. There are all sorts of birds enjoying the up-rising thermals and someone has even planted a little garden there, in a far corner. There are beautiful, sweet-smelling flowers and several fruit trees and vegetables. You want to explore but time is of the essence. Your appointment is about to arrive, so you set you tote on a nearby air conditioning unit and begin to assemble your equipment. Your appointment arrives, on time, across the street in the next high-rise building. One pop and your appointment is done.

"Goddamn it!" You exclaim softly. There is going to be a bruise on your right shoulder from the recoil. You dismantle your equipment and place the parts back in your tote and zip it.

Back down the elevator and another gentleman opens the exit door for you and you're back out into the delightful fresh air. You hum, "Another One Bites the Dust[1]," as you walk down the street and head back to your apartment. You must remember to pick up some Metamucil tablets. You are almost out of them.

[1]Lyrics by John Deacon. Sung by "Queen"

The Boomerang Shirt
Cathy Fortin-Jenkins

For three straight years, that shirt has been traveling back and forth between my husband's closet and the site of the annual Sunnymead Ranch yard sale.

This year, it was the first thing to leave the closet. It traveled at the bottom of a large grocery bag and was well hidden under some of my own tee shirts. Chuck has not worn that shirt in the six years that we have been married. He says that the short-sleeved knit shirt with a blue v-shaped stripe from shoulder to shoulder via the breastbone is too hot to wear. This shirt just hangs in the closet.

Like a boomerang, that shirt returns home. A devilish expression on his face gave him away when I noticed he was carrying a piece of crockery wrapped in knit fabric. On second glance, I said, "NOT that shirt! How he found it in the massive pile of clothing that was for sale, I will never know.

At this time, I'm not sure of its exact location, but that shirt is lurking somewhere in the garage or in his car awaiting the laundry and its triumphant return to his closet. Just what is a girl to do about that vintage-looking shirt that probably dates from the 1970s!

There is some untold story or a mystery surrounding that shirt. Someday, perhaps he will share the reasons for his attachment to that shirt.

The Cap
Stan Corella

It was the 22 of February 1968. It was a day that I would remember for the rest of my life. I had arrived at the Los Angeles International Airport (now known as LAX). I was excited to be back in my hometown. I was just so happy and had the greatest feeling of which I could not explain. My immediate thoughts were to get home and surprise my Mom. I had just arrived from Fort Lewis Washington after serving a one-year tour in Vietnam.

After exiting the airplane and making my way to pick up my duffle bag and luggage, I was approached by a young lady who appeared to be in her early 20's and was accompanied by a young man about the same age. They followed me as I went over for my belongings. She walked in front of me causing me to stop. I looked at her eye to eye. She asked me why I was smiling and why I seemed to be so delighted.

"I'm happy to be home," I answered.

She spit on the left side of my uniform. I began to walk around her and as I did the young man began to say some derogatory words and also called me a "baby killer". I continued to walk over to baggage, picked up my duffle bag and luggage. I found the nearest exit and immediately called a cab. I got assistance from the cab driver in putting my things in the cab and as I entered before closing the door, both the young lady and man continued to say things that were negative and hurtful. After entering the cab I asked the driver to drive me to my home which was in East Los Angeles.

As we were making our way to East L.A. the cabby began to preach to me. He said, "Repent and give thanks to your savior as you have sinned and have taken innocent souls from the earth."

I was stunned. I began to tear and felt like I was being jabbed by an unknown force. I held back and said nothing. There were still a few miles to go before reaching home. I realized I must stop this driver from continuing on with his preaching and so politely I asked for him to stop and change conversation. I did it with a low tone of voice and with a serious look at his rear view mirror.

"I appreciate your concern," I said, "And I realize that his holiness wants me to ask for forgiveness but before I do, I need to get home as soon as possible."

I asked him to stop at the nearest liquor store so I could buy drinks. He agreed. I made my purchase, entered the cab and told him to drop me off one block away from my home. After the driver did what I had asked, I doubled the money that was on the tab. I said my goodbye and continued down the block to my home.

Before entering the gate to my house I wiped away the tears, took a deep breath and went around to the back of the house to surprise my Mom and brothers as they had been waiting for me to arrive. I knew they would be waiting for me, but they had no idea what time I would telephone to be picked up at the airport. It was the surprise of a lifetime for my family and me. The house was full of family members, aunts, uncles, cousins, friends and neighbors. We celebrated, took pictures, sang songs, drank good drinks and ate great food.

So now and then I tell the story of me coming home. I don't hold back in telling it like it is and how for so long I had not said anything to anyone about my Army experience in Vietnam. For so many years I felt that no one would understand or even care.

Up until just recently I have been able to open up on my military experience and talk about my Army life as time goes by only because I have met with understanding professionals. I have been meeting with medical staff at the Veterans Hospital in Loma Linda, California. I meet with veterans groups and volunteers. I have also had the opportunity to meet with veterans who have shown me how to speak out and be proud. Each time we meet we share our experiences and as we do we realize these meetings should have happened a long time ago.

It feels good for each of us to tell each other what has not been said and what is on our minds and in our hearts. We share our stories not just for us, but also for those young female and male veterans of today. Veterans helping veterans is what our goal is and so in the future veterans will have some place to go and share together because in our society we tend to forget in a very short span of time.

So today, I am confronted with a combination of challenges and have been diagnosed with PTSD and physical conditions that are unexplained along with other findings of who knows what else will be added as time passes? I will continue to move on and follow through with everything I need to do and keep the faith as other veterans have shown me. We have survived for now and strive to help others to help their brothers and sisters.

I always say that I have been a lucky guy, blessed and fortunate, and give thanks that I have been able to share and tell the truth because we owe it to anyone that takes the time and interest. I am proud and in wearing the "Black Cap" a special cap which has letters that read "Vietnam Veteran, Proudly Served" and has colored ribbons across the middle signifying service in the Vietnam Conflict. I say conflict and not a war because that is what it was and it caused so much pain and suffering for so many.

I write this in honor of all who have served and the lives that have been taken. The entire conflict is still not clear and so today no real clear reason except that we did serve with honor. There were military personnel who served proudly and dedicated for love of our country. They believed in our freedom and showed the determination to survive and often held from within personal pain; yet with commitment, they arrived to a changing world.

The Foolish Virgins
Al Turnbull

Once upon a time long ago, there lived two sisters: each more beautiful, graceful, sweet, and trusting than any other maiden. Glory Anna had long black hair and eyes that glistened as shiny pieces of coal. Her voice was dulcet and so well modulated that she seemed to be murmuring lyric sonnets whenever she spoke. Her younger sister, Aurelia Belle's shimmering, golden curls rippled like lightning bolts in the slightest breeze. Her eyes were bluer than the blue of the sky or of the sea. She spoke in the tones of treasured melodies.

Their father was so charmed by his dazzling daughters that he sent servants out around the whole country to gather the finest cloth to be crafted into splendorous gowns more fashionable than any other young woman in the kingdom could afford. Their mother watched over her precious daughters and declared that no man less than a prince could be their husband.

Princes, in those times, were not as commonly available as princes seem to be today. In fact most of the princes in the realm then were old, ugly, married, or transformed by some cunning sorcerer. Those spellbound princes, were, of course, the youngest, handsomest and richest, but, alas, it was hard to find and disenchant them.

Glory Anna ventured out first and sought the counsel of a much admired astrologer who told her that she must seek a hummingbird with red feathers on its chest that glowed like a ruby in the sun. It must have green feathers on its back that sparkle like emeralds. She would have to catch the bird gently in her hand, profess her love, and kiss it on its dark black head. That might reincarnate a grateful prince who would be delighted to marry her.

Needless to say, Glory Anne hurried home to put on her newest and finest silk amber-colored gown that had a long train, which dragged behind on the ground. She forced her feet into size two tiger-hide boots, which had seven-inch heels. When so appealingly clad she rushed into the rose garden where she was certain to encounter hummingbirds. Truly, there were a few there but when trying to catch them the rose thorns ripped her marvelous dress to ribbons, and bees stung her, arousing terrible allergies. With her runny nose, tearful eyes, and cries of pain, she scared away all the birds around. She ran off to the orchard where there were many hummingbirds feeding from pink peach blossoms far up in the highest branches. The frantic girl immediately climbed far up the closest tree, destroying her wonderful boots. Grabbing at a fleet bird, she fell into the mire at the foot of the tree, resulting in mud encrusted hair. Eventually, a hummer, feeding on a sunflower growing in a patch of poison ivy, was grabbed by the filthy, exhausted girl. When she tried to kiss it, the cantankerous bird stabbed her lip with its sharp beak and flew away.

Aurelia Belle, the second daughter, sought the advice of an old hermit who lived in a cave at the top of a mountain. He suggested that she seek a prince who had been transformed into a frog. She must kiss the right frog to free the gallant young man, who, of course, would be enthralled by her beauty and finery and marry her.

Hopefully, Aurelia Belle left on her quest for the frog prince, attired in a pure white formal flock and wearing, naturally, golden slippers. She went directly to the place where frogs abide – a swamp, where she was lambasted by mosquitoes and midges, which raised terrible welts on her soft clear skin. Sloshing into the dirty water, her slippers became embedded in the mud, moreover there were horrible critters in the pool that drank her pure crimson blood. Algae growing in the ooze gave her glorious hair a ghastly green hue. The good thing for the ardent girl was that frogs were abundant and most not too difficult to catch. She kissed a number of them, a revolting experience, and one was an enchanted prince who was truly thankful for her rescuing him, but when looking at the yucky barefoot girl, dressed in muddy rags, he concluded that she was unsuited to be a royal wife.

Both bedraggled young women returned home determined to continue hunting hummingbirds and frogs in their futile quest for gallant princes who would be theirs.

MORAL: It is better to find a worthy man in a normal place rather than seeking a regal one by grabbing at tiny swift birds, with your head in tree tops, or by kissing slimy amphibians, with your feet stuck in the mud.

The Journey
Marge Ramsey

The year was 1958, when anything was possible. NASA was formed and America's 1st satellite was launched from Cape Canaveral. The 1st transatlantic passenger jetliner service began with flights between London and New York. The Ed Sullivan show was a big hit on TV and Elvis Presley was inducted into the Army. Gas was 24 cents per gallon, and the average yearly income was $4,650.

Mary was a beautiful young girl who lived with her parents in Kansas. She was an only child who had big dreams for her future. Her goal was to attend UCLA after high school graduation, study business, and see a part of the country with mountains, deserts, and beaches. To achieve that goal she said good-by to her parents and boarded a plane for Los Angeles.

Frank was a local boy, born and raised in Riverside. He also was an only child with ambitions to attend UCLA and become an electrical engineer. So at the end of summer following his high school graduation, he packed up and headed for Los Angeles.

At the beginning of the freshman year there was a semi-formal dance to give students an opportunity to meet each other and mingle. Frank walked into the room and spent a few minutes just looking around. That's when he saw her, the girl of his dreams. She was smartly dressed and sported a pair of red shoes. Her nails were painted pink, and her soft brown hair hung down to her shoulders. She was beautiful. Frank worked his way through the crowd until he reached her side.

"May I have this dance?" he asked.

"Yes you may," she responded.

He introduced himself, and learned that her name was Mary. That was the beginning of a beautiful relationship.

They dated all through college, and at the end of their junior year they each summoned their parents to visit them at school. Although they were from quite different backgrounds, Mary's family growing wheat in Kansas, Frank's living the city life in Riverside, both sets of parents hit it off with each other right away. Frank's parents adored Mary, and Mary's parents were overjoyed to meet Frank. Over dinner they announced their engagement, and their plans to marry in December 1962, after they graduated from UCLA.

On Saturday, December 15, 1962 Frank and Mary were united in marriage with all of their family and friends present. The weather turned out to be beautiful, although there was a chill in the air. The happy couple went on a short honeymoon to Las Vegas where they were given the royal treatment at the Riviera Hotel and Casino on the strip.

Then it was time to find a permanent home and settle into a daily routine of work, family time and friends. Frank and Mary had friends about their age with new babies, which made them anxious to start their own family. But children were not in the cards for them. There were not as many options for having children back in the 60's, so they ended up going through life without them. They busied themselves by getting involved with organizations that did great things for people. They helped raise funds for the American Red Cross, American Cancer Society and the American Heart Association. They were a happy couple with a love for other people as well as for each other. Mary was everything to Frank.

Throughout their working years they took many vacations together, visiting such places as the Grand Canyon, Carlsbad Caverns, Hearst Castle, San Francisco, and many more. As they approached retirement age, they made plans to travel throughout the United States and maybe take a cruise or two.

By the time they were in their mid 60's, Frank started noticing some unusual behavior being exhibited by Mary. She was repeating questions, experiencing coordination problems, and needed to be reminded of daily activities. He wasn't too concerned because these behaviors were not getting any worse. But after a few years Mary started forgetting personal history and was having trouble recognizing friends and family. He took her to see her doctor and was told that she was in stage 2 of Alzheimer's disease. This stage could last anywhere from 2 to 10 years before the disease became very severe.

As time went on, Mary gradually progressed into a more severe stage of Alzheimer's. She was confused about past and present and was having more difficulty communicating. One day Frank decided to take Mary to Coco's for dinner. She was neatly dressed in a skirt, a pretty stripped blouse with ¾ length sleeves, and sported red flats and pink fingernails, reminiscent of their first meeting. Frank was smartly dressed in jeans and a polo shirt. His glasses hung from the pocket on his shirt.

Mary said to Frank, "Where are we?" Frank told her gently that they were at Coco's.

"What are we doing here?" Mary asked.

"We are here to have dinner," Frank said.

Just as the waitress walked up to their table, Mary said, "I don't know what I like to eat."

Thank goodness for a great waitress, because she was very familiar with this couple and was quick to tell Mary exactly what she liked to eat.

Mary spent most of the time just looking down at the table. Once her food came, she ate very slowly, moving food from one side of the plate to the other between bites. There were no smiles and neither one spoke. Frank continuously gazed out the window, even while eating his food. Perhaps he was lost in memories of times past when the two of them were young and happy. He cherished Mary, even as she was slipping away. When they were finished eating, Frank picked up his napkin to wipe Mary's face, such a tender gesture. There was no response from Mary. Sadly, she was already lost to him.

The Old Man and the Ultralight

Jim Kraft

The Ultralight is a special type of flying machine. It came to be in the 1970's. People wanted to experience the joy of flying simply, safely and cheaply. The ultra light fit the bill. It had a 28ft wingspan and a length of 19ft. It was prop driven by a 45 hp engine. Far 103 regulations restrictions restrict the Ultralight to 5 gallons of gas to be treated with respect. No license or training is required but is HIGHLY ADVISABLE.

Enter the old man, me, for lessons on how to fly an Ultralight. I received flight instructions with an instructor who made my take-offs and landings survivable, but I never achieved my goal to fly solo.

I looked at my story title and hey! Remember the 1952 classic story by the gifted writer Ernest Hemingway "The Old Man and The Sea'? Can we commit literary organ transplant and make a connection?

Hemingway's fisherman and I are both old men. The fisherman's skiff became my Ultralight. The sardine bait used was my lesson fees. The 18 ft. marlin the old man caught, killed and secured to the skiff represented my total lesson investment. The tragic story ended with the sharks eating all the flesh of the marlin leaving the old man with the marlin skeleton after his terrifying ordeal at sea. The old fisherman was to regain his prestige and the respect at his fishing village with his record catch. The ending parallels my instructor informing me I could not fly solo due to age reasons and memory concerns. Hemingway's old man returned to his shack, fell asleep and dreamed of lions. I dreamed of having my own Ultralight

The Subway
Anne Hendricks-Jones

She was sitting in a New York subway car, speeding to South Ferry, where she would board one of the brightly painted orange ferries that efficiently plied the harbor to Staten Island. She had the tools of her trade in a large leather tote and an iPod in her ears, listening to AC/DC. She had an affinity for songs that hinted at her own profession, so she was grooving to "Dirty Deeds, Done Dirt Cheap[1]" and loving it. People watched her discretely, over their newspapers, chuckling to themselves at the old lady, rocking with her iPod. They figured she was listening to gospel music or something from the 30's or 40's. They were so wrong. Soon, AC/DC was done and Queen came on with "Another One Bites the Dust", and she smiled thinking of the job she had just performed. Her levity was disturbed as a bunch of rowdy, scruffy young men entered the car and took over the center aisle, as the train pulled away from Canal Street.

"Alright, listen up you assholes!" yelled one of them, dressed in a brightly colored, athletic jacket. "See these hats we're holding?" All of them had taken off their baseball hats and were now holding them out.

"We want you to put all of your valuables in here…Now! Make it snappy!"

Nobody moved. People could not believe their ears. Titters were heard. People thought it might be a street scene, an impromptu entertainment and they waited eagerly for the show to start.

"They don't believe you, Dog," said a second man, in long gym shorts, pulled down past his butt, so that white underwear was revealed.

Dog pulled out a gun from his back waistband and pointed it in a circle, around the train car.

"NOW do you believe me?" he said, maliciously.

Everyone except the old lady immediately started opening purses and reaching in back pockets. Dog posted himself at the front of the car as his partner went down and began filling his hat with cash and valuables. As the second man came to the old lady, he waited for her to move and open her tote. When she did not, he drew back to punch her. Before his fist reached her face, she reached up and caught it.

"Young man, I am old enough to be your great grandmother. While I can see that you have no respect for your elders or any people, you do NOT want to disrespect me. I have been in this world too long to be manhandled by the likes of you." And she squeezed his hand so hard, he could feel the bones crack in protest.

He could not disengage his hand but finally she released it herself and he almost fell back against the people behind him. He reached for the switchblade in his front pocket and attempted to cut her but never made it. His leg wouldn't work and when he looked down, there was a growing bloodstain just below his manhood.

"Dog!" he yelled. "Help me! She cut me!"

Dog made it halfway down the aisle but was stopped in his tracks by a bullet to his left shoulder, from her favorite little gun, kept in the sleeve of her blouse. The train was pulling into South Ferry and when it stopped, people ran screaming from the car, grabbing their stolen belongings and nearly trampling the wounded would-be hoodlums. A few stopped long enough to thank the old lady who had saved them from another New York institution.

She moved slowly from the car and approached a transit cop. "Sir," she said, querulously. "There are two gentlemen on the car who were injured as the crowd rushed out of the car. Would you see to them? They tried to rob us but the group wasn't having any of it."

The cop rushed to the car and sure enough, there were two men, lying on the floor, clearly bleeding heavily and nearly unconscious. On his walky-talky, he called for a train stoppage and EMTs. He turned to get further information from the old lady but she was gone.

"Typical," he thought. "Nobody wants to get involved!"

The Walk
Karen (Kay) Donner

I have a magnet on my refrigerator that says "Golf, a beautiful walk spoiled by a little white ball." I've played a little golf, so I am able to attest to the truth of this quote. I am one of those crazy people who enjoy this crazy game – most of the time. I get a rush out of all parts of playing golf. I like the long hits, the hits off of the hillside, the shots out of the sand, the chips and the putts. Sometimes I hit the shot just right, and I need to practice my humility, because I get such a proud feeling. Most of the time I am literally humbled by my lack of ability to hit that little white ball. Too many times I am embarrassed because my friends are watching me and I swing the club poorly. I hate to mess up, especially while people are looking.

Surprising as it is, no one has ever ridiculed me! Well, I suppose that's not exactly the truth. I am my own worst critic. Wow, can I ever make myself feel bad. When I sink into the doldrums, I can depend on one of my partners to start laughing. There is no use wallowing in self-pity, because my friends won't allow such behavior. I do the same for them. We all know exactly what is needed when we encounter one of those "bumps" on the golf course. Friends encourage each other and lovingly reduce awkward behavior to laughter.

Fortunately we are able to continue this beautiful walk that is spoiled by a little white ball. When we have completed the course, and the last ball has dropped into the cup, we rejoice in our accomplishments. We congratulate each other and plan our next outing. We usually end the day with a feast and a lot of companionship.

As I've journeyed through life, it occurs to me that there might be some similarities of life and golf. Just as in golf, life has been a beautiful walk. For both golf and life, there is a book of directions to follow and rules to uphold. No one should expect to play without knowing when, where, or how. A little white ball gets golfers into trouble, but in life, trouble can be named pride, greed, envy, etc. It's when I stumble on one of those "bumps" in life that I find my "walk" frustrating. It is so awesome that I have a "friend" who shines like a bright light, a friend who reaches down to me and takes my hand, lifts me up, and makes me smile.

I knew a long time ago that following Christ is non-negotiable. Just as my friends encourage me at the game of golf, Christ encourages me to walk the course of life. Staying in the Word keeps my heart and soul open to receive the Peace He offers. Knowing the joy of hitting the little white ball in just the right fashion isn't always going to happen. But, I will continue to try. Living a perfect Christ-like life isn't going to happen, but I will continue trying.

My golf partners and I have never hit the ball exactly the same. Our scores are always different. We start off at the same tee, end up in the same hole, but find all sorts of paths to complete the course. Isn't it the same in life? Our final objective is the prize (or the last hole) at the end of the course. We might follow different paths, stumble over different mistakes and get into various traps, but we have help getting out. We are forgiven for any of our failures as long as we yield to the hand that reaches out to save us from the dark pit of self-pity and despair.

And when the game is over, we celebrate the whole event. We congratulate one another and sit down to a feast. We look back on our game and truthfully declare we did the best we could with the talent we were given. We see each other as faithful players. And when my walk on earth is over, I pray I will be able to say that I did the best I could with the talent I was given and sit down to a feast. And I pray that I will be remembered as a faithful player.

Too Late
Mary Tourey

You came with food

Fresh water, outrage

Too late

Our homes, families

Destroyed,

You came too late.

Many died more

Are dying

Your big aeroplane,

Nice clothes came

Our outcry was

Heard too late.

Many lay dead and

More dying

Twilight
Anna Chase

The inbetween time, when light
Surrenders gently to darkness
Always subtle, often missed.

Sun slips slowly, sky to earth
Muting landscape as it glides, ever lower
Then embraced in evening's arms
Kissed gently into night.

As I linger here in twilight,
I find peace and beauty there,
Even in the word itself
Uttered softly, like a prayer
"Twilight"

Watch Dog
Al Turnbull

Oliver was not fully asleep; he was slightly alert just in case some food odor might waft about him. He was not one to let an opportunity pass by even when he was not hungry. In fact, Oliver was rarely hungry for his people looked after him well. If dogs think in abstractions, Oliver might reckon himself as well-to-do. He has fresh water always available and a nicely fenced yard which is a place with grass and ample shade trees for his exercise and comfort. Exercise is actually not a factor on Oliver's importance list. He will hurry if one of the important people summon him. He disregards the little children in the family for they are lower in the pack than his place. He tolerates them, of course; he likes everyone in his family, for, after all, he is a dog, a fine medium size fellow, dignified, not playful, and more a guardian. Oliver is a Boweimar, a cross between the Boxer and the Weimaraner purebreds.

On that particular morning Oliver was resting on the mat outside the patio door. His people had left the house, he knew, for he heard them go out to the garage and drive off. He would have liked to go with them, but he was not invited. If he recalled an event a week or so in the past, he might have been concerned about being told to get into the car, for that ride was to the vet's office where he endured being examined and suffered the pain of an injection. Going in the car was not always a joyride in Oliver's scope of things fine and dandy. Yes, he was about half asleep when a smell brought him to full awareness.

Something was on the fence in the far right side of the yard. He raised his head to catch more information. There was a flash of color, something dropped from the fence into his domain. Oliver was instantly on his feet in full watchdog mode. His people weren't here for him to call, so Oliver had full responsibility. He may not have thought of duty then, but there was something going on to spike his guarding and hunting instincts.

An audacious cat appeared on the lawn. Oliver growled to give the beast warning. It disrespected him, looked right at him, and started nonchalantly walking across the grass. This was an affront that Oliver was not going to tolerate. That creature might eat the food saved in his dish since breakfast and drink from his water bowl. Oliver knew of cats, for there was one that stayed in the house always rushing upstairs whenever he came inside. The cat in the yard smelled worse than the house cat and it was bigger and Oliver's instincts said that this one was a menace; perhaps it might even be truly dangerous. "Avoid trouble!" Oliver felt; maybe he should try to scare this thing away. He stood up showing his full height with his fur bristled, his head raised, and gave a loud warning bark. Patsy, the little terrier in the next yard, aware of the stranger's foul odor, endorsed Oliver's warning with her puny yapping.

The cat was undaunted. In fact, it growled right back at Oliver and continued to advance. Oliver was confused. It was beyond his ken that any creature would not flee when he showed his ferocity. Somehow his wolf genes were challenged, but Oliver did not have a pack to back him up as a wolf would. He was on his own and he had to do something. He did not see a need to fight; after all, that interloper looked really tough. It was making hissing sounds and its eyes were flashing. No, let it go about its business unless it started a brawl. Oliver moved out onto the grass, far on the left of the intruder, but sure not to get too close to the fence, where he might be cornered!

He did not relax but stayed on his feet, ready for anything that might happen. He was not afraid, just cautious and ready for a fight. The wildcat consumed the remaining food left from Oliver's breakfast and even had the arrogance to take a lingering drink of water.

Then came a noise: the garage door was opening and the people were home! The cat ran swiftly across the yard and jumped the fence. Just to demonstrate his courage, Oliver took a couple of tentative steps after the intruder.

The bobcat never came back; perhaps it found the city too dangerous and not as hospitable as the wilds. Oliver was always wary and alert after that encounter whenever the children were outside. True, he distained those little people who pestered him. They wanted him to play, to do dumb things like retrieving a ball. Oliver was a dog that did not like little children very much, but he knew his purpose in this family was to guard them with his life even if a lion hopped off the back fence!

When I Grow Up

Virginia Faulkner

When I was 36 I wrote about spreading hips and
sagging breasts, about gray strands that were just
beginning to appear among my brown locks, about
loneliness, missed opportunities, and the good old
days, when I was young.

Once I heard a poet who was 47 recite a poem
about old age, forgetfulness, and being shocked
when he realized he was having a
'senior moment'

I've spanned those ages by more than I care to
admit. I've been on life's rollercoaster and I'm still
riding, but with my seat belt just a little bit looser
and
Now my poems are about life, love, and what I
plan to do when I grow up.

Wind Witch

Cathy Fortin-Jenkins

Wind Witch is another name for Russian thistle. We in the West know this plant as Tumbleweed. In the 1940s, the Sons of the Pioneers made this noxious weed famous with their song "Tumbling Tumbleweeds."

The song describes a cowboy riding his horse across the undeveloped western United States. One line of the song is: "See them tumbling down, pledging their love to the ground." (Copyrighted)

I interpret this line as a romantic way of describing the tumbleweed's method of reproduction. Somewhere I read that one plant holds at least 250,000 seeds. As they are migrating or traveling across the fields and streets, they are dropping their seeds along their tumbling path. The seeds lie around in arid territory just waiting for a rainstorm to sprout the seeds. The seeds then grow into green plants with pink blooms. Then as the season becomes dry again and the winds blow, the plant detaches itself from its roots and is then free to travel where the winds blow it. The dry leafless plant is a skeletal remnant of its former self.

Across the west, all sorts of businesses carry the name Tumbleweed; there are restaurants, bands, farms, motels and ghost towns. Some brave folks even make giant snowmen out of them. One has to be fearless to tangle with the thorns of a tumbleweed.

It has become a symbol to Hollywood. Frequently, desolate, abandoned places are shown with tumbleweeds blowing across the movie screen with an accompanying sound of wind blowing.

Nikita Khrushchev of Russia once said, "We will bury you." Well, his country never did win the Cold War, but the Russian thistle is now taking over the western United States and the world. According to the encyclopedia, it first entered the United States around 1877 by way of Ukrainian farmers who imported flax seed to South Dakota. By the turn of the century or within twenty-three years, tumbleweed had reached the Pacific Coast of the United States.

Tumbleweed is an avid traveler and has now taken up residence in many countries throughout the world.

Fences and walls inhibit the tumbling and the "Wind Witches" pile up one on top of one another. To see this, take a drive down Cactus Avenue between Moreno Beach Drive and Redlands. Some of them are the size of a VW or a Toyota Camry and they are blowing into autos or even big trucks moving along at high speeds. An auto mechanic told me their sharp spines could puncture the radiator of a motor vehicle.

Last winter, I could not avoid a giant tumbler on Cactus Avenue. It crashed into my car as I was traveling fifty miles an hour. I do not know how fast it was traveling but it was a startling crash. I had to pull over while looking through the skeleton-like plant and then try to detach it. That most noxious of all weeds attached itself to the underside of my car, and I had to drive home with it dragging along under my car. I used two different rakes and a broom to knock it off onto my driveway. Then I swept it up and put it into the green trashcan. Alas, too late to prevent re-seeding! Seeing the hundreds of those wind witches this year, I know that my tumbleweed of last year sowed its seeds all across the vacant field on my street and its progenies are now on the loose and ready to pounce on me and my car.

About the Authors

Anna Chase. I grew up in the Inland Empire and raised my family here. I moved to Long Beach in 1987 and went to work for a real estate developer, where I remained for nearly 20 years. I studied real estate and management at the local community college in order to broaden my work experience. I retired in 2007, moved back to the Inland Empire and settled in Moreno Valley where I still have extended family. I'm an avid reader and enjoy playing the piano. I love to cook, especially for friends and family. I spent six years singing in an award winning a cappella chorus and another year in a gospel choir. Since joining the creative writing group, I've experimented with many types of writing, including poetry, short stories and essays. I'm still in the process of writing my biography, which starts out with childhood memories about growing up in an Italian-American family. I've also created a blog called "Lifescapes" that you can visit achaser.blogspot.com. I'm currently a member of Friends of the Library and a library volunteer in Moreno Valley.

Anna Christian is the author of six books, her most recent being *Then Sings My Soul* (2015); *Daniel's Wife*, adult contemporary fiction, (2010); *The Big Table*, an illustrated children's book, 2008; *The Newcomer (2013) and Mrs. Griffin is Missing and Other Stories*, Bobby & Sonny mystery series for preteens, (2005); and *Meet it, Greet it, and Defeat it! The Biography of Frances E. Williams, Actress/Activist*, 1999. A retired teacher, she has an M.A. in English from CSULA. In addition, she writes two blogs "Celebrating Life" on blogspot.com and a readers' blog on Goodreads.com. She facilitates a Creative Writing/Life Story class at the Moreno Valley Senior Center, and is an avid Heart & Soul Line Dancer. Her websites are anachristian.com and francesplace.org.

Stan Corella was born in Boyle Heights California, graduated
Garfield High School, in East Los Angeles, California, 1979,
and received an A.A degree from East Los Angeles College. In
1981 received B.S. degree at California State University at
Fullerton in Human Services and in 1983 received Vocational
Teaching Certificate, Bilingual Education at California State
University, Long Beach.

A Vietnam Veteran, he served in U.S. Army 1966 through
1968. After his return, he worked with various organizations,
vocational and academic training schools, volunteered in civic
and community groups to assist youth, and physically
challenged participants in need of assistance for upward
mobility. He retired from San Bernardino Community College
District as a Job Developer after twelve years of dedicated
service.

Currently he assists other veterans for needed services, a
volunteer for families in need, and he is developing training
methods for motivational support and self- development for
persons who desire to succeed.

Regina Crump was born Regina Anne Johnson in Toledo,
Ohio and raised by her father. She left home at the age of 17
for California. Longing to build a relationship with her mother,
she came with a strong will to accomplish a mission of self
worth and mending a broken family's love for one another.

She writes to heal herself and in hopes of healing others
with similar issues. Regina's vision is to continue writing
poetry and finish her first book of a mother and daughter
memoir while planning to do her family tree history which will
be her most valuable legacy. Along with those God-given
talents, she has an eye for designing fashion and has plans to
create a business that expresses the importance of health,
wellness through pampering. On her spiritual journey, she
reveals God's plans for this. She has raised two sons to
adulthood as a single parent and has one grandchild. Regina
has recently married her soul mate and is now living her life out
blissfully as Mrs. Regina Crump in God's will.

"For we are His workmanship, created in Christ Jesus unto good works, which God hath before ordained that we should walk in them." Ephesians 2:10 (KJV)

Malika Rahmaan Davis was born in Shreveport La. in 1942 in the bottom land of Louisiana. I come from a long line of preachers and from the Church of God in Christ.

I love the fact that my ancestors were Prayer Warriors, because today I feel that down through the ages, my family is still being protected and blessed because of my grandparents' prayers,

In the 1980s I opened up the first of Malika's family owned and operated Beauty Salons and Beauty Supply Stores. I am now known as the Best Hairdresser of O.C. Our family name is well-known throughout Orange County. I once had a customer of mine to return from her vacation in Africa. She came into the shop all excited and said, "Do you know you are known in Africa?" The Name Malika's. I had students from the University of Irvine to get their hair done at Malika's Hair Affair and Malika's Tricology Center. (Hair Replacement).

I am retired and now live in what I like to call MO. VAL. California.

Ollie Eubany I was born in New York, and met my husband, a Nigerian in 1958 in San Francisco. We later traveled to Nigeria where I lived for over 20 years. I wrote several articles for Nigerian Broadcasting Co. My articles were read on the radio. I am now writing my biography about my experience during the Nigerian/Biafran war.

In 1968, I was airlifted by the Red Cross from the war zone to Las Palmas and Madrid Spain. Two weeks later I was in New York. I returned to Nigeria in 1971 and wrote articles for Shell BP newsletter. I am now enjoying writing at the senior center creative writing class.

James Otis Harris Jr, is a law school graduate and law enforcement retiree. "Corey's Courtroom" was inspired by a courthouse field trip taken when he was in elementary school. "Corey's Courtroom is a series of fun stories using Corey's gifted imagination and farm animals to assist with real world problems young kids are often exposed to today. The stories are designed to assist in safely resolving conflict while keeping friendships, providing values, building confidence and developing problem solving skills.

James was born in Detroit, Michigan and grew up in Riverside, California where he met his beautiful wife and is a proud father of two children. He and his family currently reside in Moreno Valley, California. James is very active in his church, enjoys working with the youth, playing golf, sailing, traveling and learning foreign languages.

Marcia Carter-Hill was born in Los Angeles, California. She attended Thirty-Six Street Elementary, Foshay Jr. High, graduating from Manual Arts High school, all in the Los Angeles area. She is the mother of two daughters and one son, and now grandmother to seven children and great grandmother to eight young ones. Some of her hobbies are cooking, sewing, pets, and writing. Her early work career was an IBM Key Punch Operator employed by the DMV, Federal IRS, and Los Angeles Unified School District. She later attended Long Beach State College receiving an Adult Education Teaching Credential specializing in, "The Art of Dog and Cat Grooming" in 1984. She has owned and operated three pet grooming businesses, one each in Los Angeles and Orange counties, and a mobile grooming service in Moreno Valley, California starting in 1992-2007.

She has been very active with the Pet Industry and has the title of, "Certified Master Groomer" from the National Dog Groomers Association of America. She has taught, written instructions, articles, and presented seminars on this subject. She has been a dog-grooming contest Judge for many Barkleigh Groom and Kennel Expo trade shows nationwide.

150

After retiring in 2000, she joined the "Write Your Life" class at the Moreno Valley Senior Center in 2001. Creative writing has become her passion and she thoroughly enjoys recalling and writing about her life.

Cathy Fortin-Jenkins was born in Harrisburg, Pennsylvania and moved to California in 1965 by way of Tucson, Arizona. She is the youngest of ten children, so becoming the family historian was natural. She joined the Moreno Valley Senior Scribes in 2009 looking for inspiration to complete a family book she was compiling. Cathy enjoys writing about her family from stories told to her by her mother and nine siblings.

Cathy spent over thirty years working in the medical field as a Cancer Registrar. Cathy moved to Moreno Valley in 2002 from Orange County. She is active in the Moreno Valley Genealogical Society and enjoys reading and oil painting.

Anne Hendricks-Jones grew up in Baltimore, Maryland, got her bachelor's degree at Wagner College, Staten Island, New York, and her masters at California State University at Dominguez Hills, California. After two years in the Peace Corp, she traveled and worked across the United States, as a medical technologist, and finally settled down in Moreno Valley, California. She retired in August of 2013 and with her husband of 32 years, has continued traveling the United States. Anne also enjoys all types of music, especially singing, reading, writing, and cooking (sometimes).

Emma Jones's passion is with teaching how to use art as a creative tool to help heal the mind, soul, and spirit. She is the creator of Healing Art that started in her home. Healing arts reduces stress, tension, anxiety, and helps with depression. A self-taught artist who says, "art is a gift from God our Creator who gave it to me to live a more pleasant and peaceful life."

Before moving from Ohio to Moreno Valley, Ca. in 1985, Emma was the creator and owner of Montrell Marie Boutique which was an Arts and Crafts women dress making store. She was also the creator of Joy Park Pride Youth Group, a group that took pride in keeping their park and community clean. Emma has been a volunteer at several art galleries in Ohio as well as with churches, youth, adults, and women's groups. Having studied with two great artists, Jackie Allard and Stan Davis, Emma's work has been shown in art galleries and shows. She teaches Healing Arts Class at the M.V. Senior Center.

Jim Kraft is 87 years old and is fooling no one. He is an old man who knows and feels it. His amazing accomplishment is his wonderful family. His earlier background included a BSEE degree from the University of Illinois (calculators were slide rulers), and a state-side stint in the U.S. Army Air Corp, World War II. His employment career was in the aircraft industry. He now works at the job he was always destined for, a volunteer in the Cancer Clinic at Riverside County Regional Medical Center. His outlook: We're here to have fun and make you happy.

Mary Maurry professional Executive Chauffeur of 25 years retired from Boeing Space and Communications formally Hughes Air Craft Space and Communications in 2002 at EI Segundo, California. Received a degree in Graphic Arts from Platt College Irvine, California. Received a degree in Photography and Graphic Arts from Riverside Community College Riverside, California. Her photography has been featured in the Museum of Photography in Riverside, California and the Museum of Conservation near Palm Springs, California.

Mary was born in Artesia, California. Raised two children, has nine grandchildren and seven great grandchildren. Mary took this senior writing class to help her write about her heritage and childhood. She wants to share the history of generations before her and many exciting adventures as a child with family, friends and readers.

Edith Nevins - Mother of five adult children, eight grandchildren. A retired nurse of forty years. She received a B.A. in Communication. Mrs. Nevins was a community activist in several organizations in Cleveland, Ohio for over twenty-five years. She is a community activist in Moreno Valley Church as a Volunteer Tutor; secretary and member of a Christian book club; and serves on the board of Quinn Community Outreach Corporation as Secretary and Health Educator for early detection of breast cancer. "As a three-year proud member of the Life Story/Creative Writing Class, I have had many enjoyable weeks and months of writing, reading, and sharing ideas."

Marge Ramsey - I was born in Holbrook, Arizona to amazing parents. I moved to Hemet, California with my parents and two brothers at the age of four and remained there until graduating from high school and marrying my high school sweetheart, Tom. After three years of marriage, Tom and I planted our roots in "Sunnymead" in 1965 and have remained here ever since.

I had a professional career in accounting, but what I am really known for is my strength of character, and having a hand in raising four outstanding children; three natural daughters and one son adopted at the age of eight. My children will become my legacy.

I stared down lung cancer because dying didn't work for me, quit smoking after 34 years, and reprogrammed my life after the sudden death of my husband after 47 years of marriage. I have constant support and interaction with my family, and now believe I can take on any challenge life may bring my way.

C.V. Schweitzer was born on a farm south of Dodge City Kansas in 1936. Graduated from St. Mary of the Plains College 1967. He traveled the world during his thirty years in the United States Air Force retiring with the rank of Chief Master Sergeant in 1989. He is a published author, "THE MAKING OF AN ANGEL" the adventures of a lost puppy and "THUMBS" the perils of hitchhiking in 2012 and "THE SHADOW OF THE

RAINBOW" the aftermath of two shattered lives from the Viet Nam War in 2013. He is currently working on a number of short stories for further publication.

Mona Lisa Stallworth - Writing has been my preferred form of communication for as long as I can remember. This, in spite of the fact, that none of my English teachers or professors ever found my writing to be noteworthy. But, thank God, for Moreno Valley Senior creative writing class I joined last year. Here, among my fellow Senior Scribes, I found individuals that loved, understood and appreciated my writings. For me there is nothing more rewarding than to be able to share my hopes, dreams, disappointments, wisdom and words of encouragement and inspiration with others through my written words. I am a writer.

Mary F. Touray grew up in Louisville, Kentucky attending segregated school and living in a segregated neighborhood. Her life changed when her elementary school was desegregated for three years with four little white girls. This is when she knew that she and her classmates were either as smart as or smarter than those four little white girls.

Influenced by her mother Thelma, the presence of old man Zeek and her neighbor's nieces and nephew, she began reading and learning about Africa.

Her enrollment in Peace Corps sent her to Jamaica, providing her with a rich cultural experience from the Caribbean Diaspora. Taking the time to explore this rich culture, she attended plays, folk theatre and the national dance group seasonal presentations. At the same time Jamaica was a haven for the political activities of the seventies and she was able to see and hear the presentation of the Angolans when they came to meet the Jamaica Prince Minister Michael Manley to ask for the country's support at the United Nations. She was tutored by the women coordinating the commonwealth Heads of Government Conference in 1975. She was able to sit in on a presentation from C.L.R. James, and other important leaders traveling through Jamaica.

In Lesotho she co-authored a poetry pamphlet with South African refugees and influenced some policy changes in Peace Corps for the regions. She traveled through the southern African Region going to Swaziland and Botswana. In addition she visited countries in the West and East Africa.

She lived in the Gambia, West Africa from 1976 to 1999. She met her husband there and had two sons. Her life in Gambia was enriched by her, her husband and children's experience of being foster parents to children from South Africa and Namibia. When their countries became independent they all returned home from their house in the Gambia. Mary, her sons, husband, and nephew were happy and saddened by their departure.

Al Turnbull, age 89, has contributed 157 short stories, 67 nonfiction pieces and numerous poems since joining the Creative Writing Class in 2009. He is a retired school psychologist.

His interests include family, travel, and playing the organ.

155

Acknowledgements

Once again my sincere thanks to all the members of the Moreno Valley Senior Life Story/Creative Writing Class for making this publication possible. It has been my honor to facilitate this wonderful, talented and inspiring group of writers.

A special thanks to those who helped to put this anthology together - Anne Hendricke Jones for inputting many of the entries, Marcia Carter-Hill for photography, Al Turnbull and Cathy Fortin-Jenkins for editing. And thanks to all who entrusted us with your work. Special thanks to Marc Sierre, a talented artist, who not only designed the cover but also generously offered to help put the finishing touches to the project. Last but not least, the Moreno Valley Senior Center staff who have been very supportive of our efforts. *Anna Christian*

www.ingramcontent.com/pod-product-compliance
Lightning Source LLC
Chambersburg PA
CBHW071345170626
46811CB00003B/996